Praise for Bree Loewen's
Pickets and Dead Men

"[I]ncredibly compelling reading. . . . Th⟨ ⟩ engaging, honest and often painful."
—*Rock and Ice*

"This is a fine, enjoyable read . . . Loewen's prose is so disarming—at one point she says she wants her last thoughts to be about white chocolate macadamia nut cookies—you don't notice the seriousness of her trade until people actually start dying."
—*Gripped*

"A funny and sometimes cringe-inducing story of a young woman's experience as a climbing ranger where respect is hard won and on-the-job performance can be the difference between life and death. . . . With honesty, self-deprecation, and wry humor, she reflects on her experiences on Rainier: assisting injured climbers, rescuing lost children, battling inscrutable bureaucracy, lugging heavy equipment, and trying to make sense of it all. Whether it's her account of a solo climb in dicey conditions or trying to protect her good jacket while cleaning the outhouses at Camp Muir, Loewen's writing is engagingly human and humane."
—*Summit Post*

"Her engaging prose is often underscored with a reverence for the mountain on which she lived, worked, and played. Loewen's candor, utter lack of pretension, and matter-of-fact honesty make *Pickets and Dead Men* funny, poignant, and entertaining. . . . But the real value of the text isn't in the message; rather, it's in the playfulness of the stories, and in the simple bravery it took for Loewen to tell her truth."
—*AAC Journal*

"A gritty and revealing narrative from inside the belly of a tough beast, the National Park's ranger service on Mount Rainier. Bree Loewen traverses storms, tragedies, sunlit glaciers, electronic bureaucracy, and 36-hour days with humor, honesty, and a gifted pen."
—Barry Blanchard, climber, author of *The Calling: A Life Rocked by Mountains*

"In *Pickets and Dead Men*, Bree Loewen has bared her soul to reveal the character and determination it takes to show up and do your best in a man's world where the line between life and death is an everyday companion. The humble pleasures of living in the alpine world and the day-to-day drudgery of a sometimes thankless job are vividly recounted. This is a compelling read."
—Jennifer Lowe-Anker, author of *Forget Me Not: A Memoir*

FOUND

FOUND

A LIFE IN MOUNTAIN RESCUE

BREE LOEWEN

MOUNTAINEERS
BOOKS

Mountaineers Books is the publishing division of
The Mountaineers, an organization founded in 1906
and dedicated to the exploration, preservation, and
enjoyment of outdoor and wilderness areas.

**MOUNTAINEERS
BOOKS**

1001 SW Klickitat Way, Suite 201, Seattle, WA 98134
800.553.4453, www.mountaineersbooks.org

Printed in the United States of America
Distributed in the United Kingdom by Cordee, www.cordee.co.uk
20 19 18 17   1 2 3 4 5

Copyeditor: Carol Poole
Cover, book design, and layout: Jen Grable
Cover photograph: *Chair Peak in the Fall, Mount Baker Snoqualmie National
Forest, Washington State* (Jeff Goulden/iStock)

A record for this book is available at the Library of Congress

Mountaineers Books titles may be purchased for corporate, educational, or other pro-
motional sales, and our authors are available for a wide range of events. For information
on special discounts or booking an author, contact our customer service at 800-553-
4453 or mbooks@mountaineersbooks.org.

♻ Printed on recycled paper

ISBN (paperback): 978-1-68051-075-1
ISBN (ebook): 978-1-68051-076-8

Dame Cicely Saunders, the founder of the modern hospice movement once said "I asked a man who knew he was dying what he needed above all in those who were caring for him. He said: 'For someone to look at if they were trying to understand me.' Indeed, it is impossible to understand fully another person, but I never forgot that he did not ask for success but only that someone should care enough to try."

CONTENTS

AUTHOR'S NOTE

I WRITE SO I CAN sleep. I know I'm writing other people's stories. I know it's my job to listen, just to be there, and I can never speak for someone else or know another person's experience. So for a long time, once I'd written the stories I burned them in the fire pit in my backyard and scattered the ashes. Or I turned the paper into boats and floated the words out into Puget Sound, committing what had happened to the universe to remember.

But the thing is, for twenty years I've been amazed by how kind the outdoor community is, how often I see people reaching out to each other, creating a thoughtful chapter in history for this small spot on the map. So now I've changed my mind about what I should and shouldn't do. In the most respectful way I can, and with the goal of fostering human connection, I've kept some of my writing, and hope other people read it.

This was my experience, what I heard, what I did. In that way, all descriptions, events, and dialogue described in these pages are based on my personal memories, documentation from Seattle Mountain Rescue's mission reports, and discussions with other participants. Any errors or misinterpretations are mine alone. I have also taken certain liberties with chronology in the hopes of creating a more cohesive narrative.

I'm also worried that I say "I" too much, so given this chance, I want to state unequivocally that doing mountain rescue and parenting are both utterly collaborative work and if I have not mentioned my partners enough, know that all of you have my upmost respect and I would be lost without you.

In case you want to find out more about Seattle Mountain Rescue to comment, donate—or even better, join—here's how to contact us:

Seattle Mountain Rescue
P.O. Box 67
Seattle, WA 98111
www.seattlemountainrescue.org
www.facebook.com/seattlemountainrescue/

PEBBLE CREEK

I'M STANDING AT THE TOP of Pan Point in a snowstorm. I walked two and a half miles and gained about 2,000 feet of elevation to be here at this spot, still low on the flank of the mountain. As I look out, the view is both familiar and eerie, like a complicated painting on the far side of the room, always noticed during a friend's dinner parties.

Russell and I are taking turns rescuing people. I do a rescue and he stays home with Vivian, and then he does one and I make waffles for dinner, and Vivian and I watch *Phineas and Ferb,* which she's really too young to watch, but I let her do it anyway because she likes Perry the Platypus and because Dr. Doofenshmirtz reminds me of my friend Aaron, who, sadly for me, left SMR and ended up as a doctor in Zimbabwe after a series of strange life experiences. After Vivi goes to bed I fill out job applications and listen to Broken Bells's "The Ghost Inside" on continuous loop.

And then it's my turn again. So on Tuesday I'm taking a photo of a blood-encrusted yellow Italian leather boot at the top of Pan Point, trying not to get the blocky outline of my phone's shadow with my headlamp behind it centered in the picture. I'm planning to use the photo when I give mountain safety talks. I hate doing talks with stock photos.

It's midnight at around 6,700 feet on the south side of Mount Rainier and a snowstorm's in progress, but it's only a moderate, strangely warm sort of snowstorm. Even after an hour in this one spot with the snow blasting off the black ice and grey striated rock, forcing tendrils into my clothes, only now can I feel my buttocks starting to join the rest of my body in a coordinated shivering effort.

The park rangers at Mount Rainier normally do their own rescues, but they're short staffed in the winter, so they called out mountain rescue groups—Seattle, Olympic, and Tacoma—to take care of this minor incident. Tacoma Mountain Rescue provided the doctor, Olympic ran the thing, and we—Seattle—brought in the technical gear. We planned it all out in the parking lot. Now, in a bit I'll be running the rigging iterations, lowering the man who owned the boot down from Pebble Creek along the icy snowfield and back to the parking lot in Paradise, as soon as TMR's ER doc and the flight nurse, just back from his fourth tour of duty in Afghanistan, finish splinting the guy's leg and get him into the litter. I'm taking pictures with my phone, listening to the crew jostling around like puppies and yelling back and forth over the wind. It's taking them a while to get the man into the litter since I guess the leg injury is an open fracture with little bone fragments, and apparently stuff needs to be irrigated, and movement is difficult.

He was hiking by himself, wearing ice walkers on his boots, descending from Camp Muir through rocks and a mixture of snow and ice when he slipped, slid about fifty feet grappling with the snice, and then jammed his foot into a rock in order to stop. He stopped.

Some really awesome skiers found him first. They were awesome just to have tried skiing when there was more gravel than snow, but also because they had a radio, and contacted the Park Service with the injured hiker's location. Then they'd stayed for the rest of the day and into the night, kept him warm and cared for him, which is really unusual and wonderful, especially given that it was quite windy. The skiers stayed until we showed up, which took a long time because of the drive. Mount Rainier is a three-hour drive south from my house in Carnation, but then, the park is a long way from anywhere, really. I called Russ on the way down to say I didn't think I'd be home by five in the morning, when he has to leave for work, and so he drove Vivi over to his mom's for the night.

We got to the parking lot at Paradise around 10 p.m. and started heading up the mountain. On the way up I had my crew of Seattle Mountain Rescue guys scout our descent route, planning when we needed to lower and finding our anchor spots to match the length of our extra-long rescue ropes.

Now, finally done with the picture of the boot, I refocus past the brilliant white snowflakes, blazing repetitive flashes in the light of my headlamp, to see a huddle of climbers in a place that dampens light and sound and feeling.

This is a strange, monochromatic, expansive place above Pan— people walk through it to get to Muir or beyond. It feels vaguely ominous, not technical or towering, but flat and black and, with the snow falling like brush strokes, roughly impressionistic. The sheer volume of the cold so easily leaves those who come here obtunded, forced to sleep, too numb to get away. This is where my friends are tonight, huddled together in a space as large as a bivy bag behind a rock, working to offset that effect. They are a noisy, mismatched, ridiculous bunch of craftsmen with complementary skills who are not being paid to do this job. The more I think about it, the more I think this is the only way to escape the numbness, by shocking it with our crazy mix of personalities and backgrounds and pants colors.

I brought with me several people in brightly colored pants, plus Bob. Bob retired too early, first from the Marine Corps and then in a few other branches of the service. He does not condone hot pink pants. He has retained the cropped haircut, and lists his hobbies as climbing and golf, both of which he does with great proficiency. On several occasions, while getting food after rescues, he has bought the whole table dinner, telling the waitstaff that we're his children.

Now, Bob is trying to get the injured hiker, who is also an ER doctor, to sit on his sleeping pad for insulation. Bob just took an EMT class and he wants to work the lingo, and he's yelling above everyone else, over and over, "Get the pad under your ischium!" "No, higher, under your ischium!" "Just sit on it so it's under your ischium!"

The flight nurse finally turns to Bob, waving his blue nitrile gloved fist in the air. "Say ischium one more time and you'll get my metacarpals in your mandible!"

I can't see Bob's face, but I know his eyes slant behind his custom safety sport bifocals, and then they all dive back behind the boulder, and I just smile in the dark, watching them.

Mount Rainier is beautiful at night, looking down the end of the big trees, low on the mountain and early in the winter, heather totally encased in ice mushrooms. I love the clear ice. I love the way the palms of my gloves and the knees of my pants stick to it. I love when it is cold enough that the snow blasting at my jacket doesn't leave damp spots. The dryness is such a blessing.

This rescue is so much more straightforward than anything I've done in ages. It feels fun to have an easy plan and a strong crew, with no real suffering on our part. I wish I'd brought glow sticks just so I could see the line of anchors below me like lights on an ice runway, smooth and mellow and perfect—except for the rocks, which I know are there—but still it looks perfect from where I stand, looking at the slope dipping down Pan and out to Paradise. I can see my crew below me in the dark, ready to start lowering the man, bickering about who gets shotgun on the way home. They're all crazy to argue, because it's me. Actually . . . now that I think about it, it probably isn't. Paul hates driving at night, and I've always been a good anchor-leg driver. But anyway, really, this is good service. Who gets their leg splinted in the middle of nowhere, in the middle of the night, for free by half an ER's worth of folks who enjoy working together this much? I sense my friend Myers from Olympic smiling in the dark to my right for exactly the same reason I am. Sometimes volunteers can be iffy. It's tough to know who you're getting. But sometimes volunteers can be awesome, and tonight I know we're awesome.

"You guys ready yet?" I yell over.

"Yup," says Myers, "it's yours. Go for it."

Once we get the injured hiker back to Paradise, I end up riding to Ashford, the tiny town just outside the park boundary, in the National Park Service's aid car along with the man and the flight nurse from Madigan; the park's EMT drives. We get there at three-thirty in the morning. Ostensibly I'm here to assist the nurse in case he needs it, but I just hold the biohazard bag where he wants it, and grab towels. It's really warm in the aid car. It feels amazing. Cozy. Like I'm already dreaming, and in the dream I'm in a diving bell traveling through dark water. A long time ago I worked as an EMT, and I used to sleep in the empty ambulances between shifts. The garbage can fills up with bloody towels. I tie up the bag and reline the can. I make it tight with the knot underneath the top edge. I love a tight trashcan liner. The three of us talk about skiing.

When we originally called the Ashford Fire Department they said we could meet them at their station, and they'd take our injured hiker to the hospital of his choice in Seattle, but when we arrive they tell us that they're exhausted because of a fatality accident—someone crashed a car in a lake earlier in the evening. So now they say they'll take him to meet a private ambulance company in South Hill, the same one I used to work for, and those guys can take him the rest of the way. It seems complicated to me, but the park EMT says he can't go farther than Ashford. We transfer the hiker from one aid car to another, and then the park EMT waves, backs out, and heads back to Paradise. The Ashford Fire Department crew takes off with the hiker toward South Hill.

All this time on the way from Paradise to Ashford the SMR truck has been trailing us, waiting to pick me up but far enough back that I don't see them, along with another car full of the rest of the Tacoma guys. The Tacoma car pulls over in front of the cinder-block fire station's empty bay doors after the transfer so they can get their nurse back. As the nurse piles into the tiny sedan, the SMR truck blows past us, still following an aid car . . . just a different one.

"Dudes!" I say, "My homies just left me! I bet Paul is driving." Paul is a half Filipino, half Dutch programmer with beautiful calves and a ponytail, and married to a neuroscientist and quilting expert who will be upset that he was gone all night. Paul also wears glasses. I explain that Paul doesn't have great night vision. Usually, I drive at night.

"Get in," the Tacoma guys say. "We'll chase them down." There are five of them plus gear in the sedan. I dive across their laps in the back seat. The shocks in the sedan max out as we rocket up and down, honking and flashing our lights. There's no cell phone service anywhere near Mount Rainier, and we have to catch up before the

TMR's route diverges or else I'll be stuck going to the City of Destiny, two hours south of Seattle, with nothing but the clothes on my back.

Finally, we get Paul to pull over, and I drive the rest of the way home. It's breakfast time when I walk in the door, seven in the morning on Wednesday. The house is strangely quiet since Vivian is at her grandma's. Russ has long since gone to work. My mother-in-law Debbie is going to drop Vivi at preschool at nine. Walking Vivi to school means holding her little hand so I can lift her out of potholes where the water would overrun her ladybug rain boots, and I'm sad to miss it today, but the rest of the mornings are so frenetic with inevitable wardrobe crises and snack-packing conundrums, the quiet is nice, too.

I open the refrigerator door. We're out of milk. Russ must not have been able to eat cereal for breakfast this morning. He's probably hungry right now. I rummage around and find bread and zucchini and one egg. I slide some bread in the toaster and start making a zucchini omelet that's mostly zucchini.

Today, I need to go grocery shopping, and I also need to figure out what to do with my life, and start working on that profession's application process. I've been a stay-at-home mom for four years. Crazy. I like being a stay-at-home mom because it gives me the time to be there for my family and my community when they need support in between getting the car's oil changed and buying vacuum cleaner bags, and I tote around Vivi, trying to teach her how to be a good person at the same time. But it's also been a bit of a struggle. Russ is pretty self-sufficient, so the only things he needs me for, the things that count as worth doing, are the tangible things: folding laundry, making sure the dining room table isn't sticky and there are no toys visible when he comes in the front door. Russell does in fact suffer from OCD. If there's a fuzzball on our hardwood floor, his eye starts to twitch, but he's remarkably even-keeled with the big stuff in life. I think the attention to detail comes in handy on complicated rescues— and for his job as a superintendent for a construction company. He just spent nine months overhauling the mental health center for Swedish Ballard Hospital. I'm told it's a beautiful space—the lights adjust over the course of the day to match a human's natural circadian rhythms, the entryway pillars are imported Italian tile, and the showerheads are flush to the ceilings, leaving nothing for folks to hang themselves on. He does amazing work and, just as he works with his guys to keep his job site clean and organized, he's focused on getting me and Viv to keep our house really clean. He spent ten years painstakingly restoring our house to 1930s glory. Of course, it's impossible to keep an occupied space immaculate, especially with a kid, but we try.

But I can't handle the idea that the greatest success I'm capable of, where I should be focusing, isn't on helping people or increasing the community's happiness, but on stuff like making sure there are absolutely no toast crumbs on the floor. I mean, I clean the floor, so most of the time it's more of an ideological conflict over priorities. But that doesn't make it less of a conflict. Russ is pretty sure that it's time for my vacation from real life to end. We both agree that it will help our marriage if I get a real job so I can work for someone else. So he fired me from being a stay-at-home mom. This is the first time I've ever been fired, and it was jarring since I've always been an over-achiever. Finding another job with homemaker on my resume has been a slow process.

I might have protested more, but most of my friends share Russ's sentiment. I don't have any stay-at-home mom friends. I don't really know any moms at all. There are no other active moms in Seattle Mountain Rescue, working or otherwise. Most of my friends are in SMR and have at least one master's degree, and a good cross-section have PhDs, and are either engineers or in business running large swaths of major corporations, or are physicians, and are guys. Good guys, but still guys who don't think that being a full-time mom counts as having a job. They tell me good-naturedly that I'm smart enough that I should really be doing something important with my life. But at the same time, the only reason I know them is because they sacrifice sleep to go help carry injured people out of the woods for free, too, and they're amazing at it. Even Russell does this. It's like a secret life of compassion and altruism that no one can bring themselves to admit to. Funny.

I sit down at the dining room table with my zucchini omelet, surrounded by old wood-framed windows. In the summer, there will be honeysuckle in these windows, but for now only the brown vines are visible in the pale winter light. There was a woman—a florist—who lived in our tiny Craftsman-style cottage for its first fifty years. She

planted white dogwoods and lilacs, white peonies and rhododen-
drons, all ancient now. After Vivian was born, I made friends with
the lady who runs the historical society in Carnation, and she told me
the florist's name had been Vivian, too. But really, Russell bought the
house before we were married, because he knew he could restore it,
and because it's close to the mountains; and I'm sure the rest of it is
coincidence. It wasn't, like, fate that we're where we should be in this
world. I need to send out another batch of resumes.

Ten hours and four minutes and one grocery shopping trip later
we get called out for an ice climber who fell thirty feet after his anchor
failed somewhere at Alpental, which is a ski area fifty miles from Seattle, but it's also the name of the whole mountainous valley where the ski
area sits. This valley runs north to northwest at the top of Snoqualmie
Pass, creating a three-sided canyon. Along the west side is Chair Peak,
on the east side are Guye Peak and Mount Snoqualmie. This ice
climber is somewhere up in the valley beyond the ski area, supposedly
between Mushroom and Big Trees, two backcountry ski runs.

Nobody from SMR is required to respond when we get a call. If
we can drop what we're doing and go, we do. When the personal sacrifice of those hours would be too great because it's our kid's birthday,
or we're going out to dinner with our parents, then we usually don't.
Except when we get a follow-up phone call saying that not enough
people are coming, and then. . . .

After almost twenty years doing search and rescue, I've gotten
a feel for how many people and how much time a rescue is going
to take. Sometimes I'm wrong, but usually it takes one rescuer four
hours, in the dark and with good cell phone coordinates, to find and
retrieve a hiker who has gotten lost on the Mailbox Peak Trail. It takes
a minimum of twenty people to carry out an injured trail runner
from near the top of McClellans Butte during a windstorm.

Sometimes I underestimate, like when Russ and Larry, SMR's
chairman—corporate mastermind from MIT and wearer of polo
shirts with the collars up—and I were headed up to do a Tooth climb
to watch the sunset. We ran into an older lady sitting in the dirt and
crying a mile and a half up the trail to Snow Lake. Next to her was
a red emergency tarp with a brown scraggly tail sticking out from
under it. After a couple minutes of trying to figure out what to say,

and still hoping we'd be able to get our climb in, we asked her if her dog had died, and if so, did she need help carrying him back to her car? She said yes with unusual quickness, and pulled back the tarp to show us her deceased 175-pound Irish wolfhound, already stiffening with rigor. After one and a half miles, it took everything we had to get the dog into the back of her Prius. Then we turned around and headed back up to the Tooth. Needed more people.

Sometimes a rescue takes quite a few folks, and I can tell when we don't have enough people coming. I get acutely more worried when I'm at home making waffles, like I was that Wednesday evening, and have time to obsess over it.

It was Russell's turn to go, so he took off toward Alpental to go help the ice climber with anchor failure. In between melting butter and helping Vivian separate eggs for the waffles I started calling the roster, hoping to scrounge up more people, but everybody knows my number and they know if they pick up the phone, I'll rope them into scrapping their evening plans and staying up all night. Which is fine, once. Or twice. But now, lots of people don't pick up because they know that when you lose your life-balance, when you suddenly realize your daughter doesn't expect you to read her a bedtime story anymore because she just assumes you won't be home, or when your fridge is empty, then you're just as lost as the next twenty-something in yoga pants who went hiking to see the sunset and didn't bring a flashlight.

After I had tried everyone with last names A through O, MattyP answered his phone. I told him he had to go because the team needed him. The texts from the King County Sheriff's Office said thirty-foot fall, two broken legs, and going into shock. They needed an EMT to be there right now. I told him that the EMT was him.

"Okay," he said. "I'm going."

I know that, even though it's hard to answer the phone, there is something awesome about having the person on the other end tell you about a life-or-death emergency where the team needs you, immediately, to stave off unimaginable disaster. I enjoy making this phone call as much as I suspect the people on the other end of the phone enjoy receiving it. "Godspeed," I tell MattyP. He fumbles the phone, hangs up. I fold the egg whites in with the rest of the batter, and plug in the waffle iron.

I feel proud of myself. Russ, Taylor, Drew, Jenn, Larry, Patrick, MattyP, and a few more SMR people head off into the end of an early December cold snap. It's only 5 p.m., but Vivian likes to eat early, and it's pretty much totally dark at five these days. We eat on the kitchen floor surrounded by confetti; Vivian is obsessed with cutting construction paper into smaller pieces of construction paper. Her teacher says using scissors helps with hand-eye coordination.

When he crawls into bed early the next morning, Russell tells me that the ice climber's belayer had called for help. There had been terrible cell phone service, so nobody had been able to pinpoint his coordinates. The partner had tried to put some insulation under the fallen climber, and then left to see if he could get a call out and help guide folks back to the spot.

Russell and Taylor had gone together, following the ice climber's partner, and he'd led them up a frozen slime- and moss-filled drainage that was maybe trying to turn into an ice climb, but wasn't quite there yet. Taylor's a former geologist, still in his twenties. He recently committed both to staying local, by tearing up his passport, and to getting his MBA before he turns thirty. And he's a really fluid, beautiful climber.

Russ told me that everything in the drainage was covered by just enough snow to make it irritating and slow. After a long time, getting fairly high up, the partner realized that they must have left the trail too early. They were in the wrong drainage altogether.

"Not great downclimbing," said Russ. "And how can your partner forget where he left you?"

"I imagine he was pretty stressed," I said, thinking about it.

"I would never do that," said Russ, rolling away from me.

"Leave someone?" I asked.

"Forget where I put something," said Russ.

"I know," I said, patting his back.

Meanwhile, MattyP, Larry, and Patrick—committed Pacific Northwest whiteout skier and owner of three degrees in awesome-sauce and one in mechanical engineering—carried up a backboard, litter, ropes, rigging material, oxygen, and a variety of other stuff. It was dusk when they started hiking in. As soon as Russ called on the radio to let them know he wasn't in the right gully everyone realized that they actually had no idea where the injured climber was so they started yelling to see if they could hear him yell back. Just past Mushroom they could hear someone shouting in the distance. As they got closer, they realized that the injured climber was lying on a narrow bench between two ice steps. Larry and MattyP rappelled down to him, leaving Russ—once he made it back down the drainage—to communicate with base and give the GPS coordinates to the incoming helicopter and the rest of the teams. MattyP was, in fact, the only EMT there, and he had to work alone at first while Larry coaxed a mess of cams into an icy crack and equalized them with a picket so they could secure themselves and then keep the climber from sliding off the lower ice step while they got him onto the backboard. The helicopter finally arrived and whisked the climber away, and then everyone picked up their stuff and hiked back out.

I found out later that MattyP had been at work teaching physics at Seattle Prep when I'd called him. He'd left so fast that he had forgotten his wallet on his desk, which would have been mostly okay, except that halfway to Alpental he was suddenly stuck with the gas pump nozzle in his empty tank. His car's gas light had been on since that morning, almost thirty miles ago in Seattle. He knew that if he kept going, it was unlikely he'd make it to Alpental, and there was absolutely no way he could get there and then back again. But he had no time to think about it—the crew would leave without him. Someone was going to die if he didn't get there. So he figured that his car would just make it because it had to, and he'd deal with the rest later. While they were hiking out after the climber was rescued, MattyP asked Russell if he could borrow twenty bucks for gas. Russ lent him the cash.

There is a gas station at the Summit, only a mile or two from Alpental, along with the Summit Central ski area and the Pancake House, and not much else. At midnight in December, it was all deserted. MattyP coasted gratefully in, only to realize that the gas station building was closed, and you need a credit card in order to pay at the pump.

After MattyP had sat in his cold car for five minutes without a plan, Patrick fortuitously rolled up to get gas too, so MattyP walked over and asked if he could borrow Patrick's credit card. In exchange,

MattyP said he'd buy Patrick dinner at McDonald's in North Bend with Russell's twenty bucks on their way home, since they were starving, and nothing much else is open in North Bend in the middle of the night. Patrick said that would be great since it was actually his birthday, and he'd appreciate a little party.

So they both got gas and then headed to McDonald's, where they ran into Larry, already in line. MattyP said he would buy everybody dinner, except he was a little short on cash—for three people and all—so Larry gave MattyP twenty bucks, MattyP bought dinner for everybody, and then they sat and had a birthday party for Patrick.

After Russ got home on Thursday morning, it was six whole days of quiet before Paul, Garth, and Steve spent sixteen hours trying to get an injured trail runner off a rocky promontory near the summit of McClellan Butte. Sleet blew sideways, and KCSO's helicopter pilot decided it was too dangerous to fly. Paul found himself holding the injured man, keeping him from sliding off the exposed ridge crest with one hand while trying to hold a tarp over both of them for what turned into hours. Meanwhile, the rest of the crew got shuttled through the Cedar River Watershed, past high-security gates and down two hours' worth of marginal dirt roads before they could even hike up the back side of the peak to get to this obscure spot. It was almost midnight when they started lowering the critically injured runner off a rock horn, down a series of steep ledges, and over a scree field before finally getting him back to the dirt road at five o'clock, and into an aid car around seven.

Technically, it had been my turn to go, but our parents were coming over for dinner, which is kind of a big production since Russ's parents are gluten-free pescatarians with restrictions, my dad won't eat sugar and is flirting with going paleo, and my mom will eat whatever as long as there's homemade strawberry rhubarb pie for dessert. The real kind, which must include gluten, sugar, and a trending Pinterest crust design. Vivian's only eating macaroni and cheese, Indian food, and cereal these days, so making a family dinner is complicated. Weighing the severity of the consequences of bailing on dinner to go on a rescue, I realized I couldn't. So I didn't. I tied on my favorite apron—the one with tiny red cherries on it—and started prepping. I enjoyed the challenge, but I could feel the phone in my pocket buzzing, text after text looking for more people, and I knew what that meant.

Paul called me the next day, and said he'd gotten home at breakfast time. He's married with two kids. He'd sat down for breakfast and started randomly weeping into his cereal bowl, just over the stress of the whole thing, and he wanted me to tell him if that was normal. What's normal is a question I'm totally unqualified to answer. But I love working with folks who really care about other people, who put their whole selves out there even if it's a secret, even if that means having to switch to oatmeal for breakfast because oatmeal only gets better with a little salt in it.

GRANITE

RUSS HAS JUST AGREED TO throw my duffle bag in his truck and leave it at the trailhead. I hang up and jam my phone back into my pocket. I'm at my mom's house in Bothell. I was dropping off a strawberry galette, but now unexpectedly I'm dropping off Vivi, too. I contemplate not going.

"You don't have to go on every rescue," Mom says, looking aggrieved. She's an artist. She's already dressed for a gallery shindig she was planning on leaving for in a few minutes. It's the same thing Russ told me when I called him to see if he could toss my gear in his truck on his way out the door of our house, heading to the same rescue.

Russell and I have been married for eight years. I met him in Explorer Search and Rescue, part of the Boy Scouts at the time, when he was sixteen and had a pageboy that he kept out of his face with a bandana. Now in his mid-thirties, he's still got the bandana. I was first attracted to him because he skis and climbs and likes hiking foothills in the rain, like I do. I have a fear of abandonment, and can never leave the Pacific Northwest, and Russ was as much in love with this place as I was. I remember that his mom, Debbie, invited all of us in ESAR leadership training over for Easter dinner one year, and the easy-going atmosphere was so Norman Rockwell I just wanted to fall asleep on the sofa. I couldn't please my parents during those years, and I remember that ten minutes after I first met her, I asked Debbie if she'd adopt me. I had a couple of friends in the Worldly Philosophers and Dismal Scientists Club and we spent a lot of time trying to come up with a decent ontological argument for God's existence, even though only two of them believed in God. But Russ had a group of friends who made bets about whether they could go an entire year eating only things that they had barbecued. I did not find what I was looking for, but they did figure out how to barbecue pizza and pancakes, and grilled everything for twelve months, although the next year they all went vegetarian. He just seemed so well adjusted and geared for success.

Russell has been doing search and rescue since he was fourteen; Caley taught him. In his fifties now, Caley is an unflappable engineering manager for a Fortune 500 company. For work, he wears ugly penny loafers with tassels, but he has been doing search and rescue and spending his free time in the woods since he was fourteen, too. Together he and Russ have a detailed, meticulous mental inventory of every trail, every drainage, and every accident in recent memory. They enjoy managing incidents together enough that they're still doing it twenty-some years later.

Debbie has spent her whole adult life dealing with Russell and his midnight exploits—and his two brothers, and their exploits. Since she is already used to having her plans disrupted, and has a Rockwellian desire to spend time with her grandchild, I can usually get her to babysit Vivian with no notice.

Now my mom and I are closer than we were, but she's torn about on-call babysitting because she grew up a daughter of the '70s. She's an artist, and a free spirit, and she loves Vivi, but she doesn't like the idea of staying home and babysitting while everybody else is out having adventures. I think part of it is that our culture just doesn't put much emphasis on the importance of caring for children—the very act comes with social stigma in an anti-women's lib kind of way. And I don't blame her. I hate the stigma, too. That's half the reason I spend so much time trying to come up with one career or another. I need some job that actually means something, that comes with status and money and power over my own destiny, while trying to tow Vivi and the rest of my life along behind me.

But I really need my mom to watch Vivi so I can go on this rescue. . . . I have to keep my friend network together. It's easier to maintain closer ties when we see each other frequently—and it always feels like it's been ages since I've had any adult interaction. I feel that moms say that as a joke, but I don't actually know very many other moms; we never seem to have much in common, and social isolation doesn't seem funny to me. Even after just one or two days without speaking any words aloud to another adult, with just Russell's voice in my head, maintaining a constant running commentary on the lack of progress on whatever I'm cleaning at the time, I start to feel like I'm being suffocated by my own withering self-concept; every time I breathe in, I'm just sucking it in tighter around me.

Also, I think shared hardship increases camaraderie, which is what I want the most out of this world. What if something miserable happens on this mission and I miss out on it? I can't stand the thought. Plus, I like running things. Working with people. I like bringing order from chaos, the more complex the problem, the better.

The text says there's a man having a heart attack on top of Granite Mountain, so somebody—possibly someone I know, as I'd say close to half the people we rescue we know personally one way or another—will die if I don't go. Or maybe he'll die anyway, even if I do go. Or maybe if I don't go, someone else will go instead and they will do everything I would have done and it won't matter that I didn't go.

"Your hair looks awesome!" I tell my mom, eying the Macklemore cut and new red color. "Very hip." Amazing that she can actually pull this stuff off in her sixties. I couldn't have done it in my twenties. "Also, that shirt makes you look thinner. Also, I'll be back tonight." The hair is good. I'm not actually convinced on the strategically ripped shirt, and I'm totally sure I won't be back tonight.

"I have a lot to do," she says, sounding uncertain, "and I've had a headache for two weeks and it's left me totally exhausted. Could you be back in four hours?"

"Maybe," I tell her, and she knows I won't be back, and I know she knows; it's a tacit acceptance on her part without losing face by explicitly giving in to my request. I know she's watching Vivi again because she loves me. Because she likes playing with Vivi, and she just can't say so.

Vivian doesn't say goodbye to me anymore. She's wandered into the living room to the Tinker Toy stash. I follow her in and try to hug her, but she's stiff. She usually comes back from one grandma's or the other saying she had a good time though, so I don't think she's too upset. But I don't have time to investigate. I start backing slowly toward the door. With every minute, my crew will be farther and farther ahead. Already, there's no way I can catch them.

When I get to Exit 47 and the Granite Mountain trailhead, six miles before Snoqualmie Pass, the parking lot is wet and the cloud deck is super low. The top of the mountain sits higher than the level of the pass, and everything from here into Eastern Washington is totally socked in. No helicopter today. Most of my crew is already gone, I can see their cars scattered in the lot. It's five in the afternoon. Wes was already close to the trailhead when the call went out, and he started hiking within minutes. Taylor and Jarek—a super-thin Polish engineer and coach for youth climbing competitions—had been sport climbing nearby at Exit 38, so they probably got here within minutes, too. As I pull up, I can see Russ and McCall jogging toward the trailhead with their packs on, and Larry is somewhere up the trail in between everybody else because I can see his car, but I can't see him.

Ed, the King County sheriff's deputy designated to oversee all SAR operations in the county, is standing next to his truck talking to Eric, the guy directly in charge of the ESAR folks. We get a random assortment of other deputies when Ed's not on duty, but mostly we get Ed. He's the only one here getting paid, but even though he's technically in charge, he runs interference for us a lot more than he ever tries to tell us what to do. Or figure out what we're doing. Ed's in his fifties, with spiky salt-and-pepper hair and an intense personality. He's poised to retire but I don't think he will, since I'm not sure he owns any clothes besides his black jumpsuit and gun belt. And I think he's a good detective. It seems to me that retirement is often not as good as the feeling of doing the thing that you're good at.

"Is there anything left to take up the trail?" I ask Ed and Eric and the knot of guys with maps and radios and orange vests.

"No" says Ed, "everything's gone up already."

There isn't any urgency in the atmosphere between them today. Maybe there was earlier, but now they must be confident that enough people have gone out. I want to leave the parking lot, to hike after my crew. I can't catch up with them, but I can get there sooner to help out if they need an extra pair of hands.

"Bree, come here," orders Ed. "I want to show you these pictures from this thing from a few weeks ago. I'm going to use them in my crime scene classes."

"I don't want to, Ed, I've seen them. I took them, remember?"

"Oh yeah," says Ed. "Come look at them anyway." It was documentation for a report on a man who tried to die by simultaneously shooting himself, tumbling down a cliff, and drowning in the lake at the bottom. Because, well, who can really say why? Anyway, he died. I don't really want to look again. But staying on Ed's good side is a good thing. He gave me a body bag for my birthday. It was a fine gift. I used it.

Ed used to be a K9 officer; his dog could eat a metal folding chair. He took the SAR gig when his dog retired. I know the dog died recently, and now Ed's telling me a story about how he shot a man at point blank range as he started to slit his girlfriend's throat. It was the third person Ed had killed. I've heard this story at least twenty times. Ed said drinking wasn't the answer so he took up gourmet cooking to fill the lonely hours alone with his memories and without his dog.

There's a wild cat that lives behind Ed's house. He lives way out in the woods, and I'm picturing a bobcat softly padding behind an abandoned, moss-covered dog igloo in his backyard.

"I've been grilling wild king salmon with a little lemon and butter on cedar planks," Ed says, "and I leave half of it out on my back deck and the wild cat will come out of the woods. I can see it from inside the kitchen window approaching the deck and then if I'm really quiet, she will come and eat the fish."

How big is the cat? Eric wants to know. Ed shows with his hands. Eric and I look at each other knowingly.

"What color is the wild cat?" I ask.

"Feral cat" says Eric. "Not wild cat, feral cat." I tell Ed that he can grill some salmon for me.

Eric thinks maybe the guys already hiking up could use another sleeping bag, and he gives me his personal 700-fill goose down bag from one of the gear bins he has stacked in the trunk of his Subaru. Nobody likes to use their own sleeping bag on a rescue. Sleeping bags get bloody or peed in. Even if the bag looks and smells fine afterward, you always associate it with this memory of confusion and trauma every time you start to fall asleep. Russ didn't throw mine in the truck, so it's not an option. Eric must be pretty confident that we won't need his. He's just humoring me, giving me something to take, but I'm grateful. I want to feel like I'm carrying something purposefully up the trail, so I stuff it into my backpack and start jogging by myself.

Granite is not a climb, it's just a hike. It has about 3,800 feet of gain and it's so familiar. I've done dozens of rescues here, but mostly I hike Granite at night for exercise because it's fairly close to my house, and it's beautiful. It's a good ski in the winter, and no matter if I take the trail, or one of the chutes, or meander up a ridge in the summer, the way is thick with lupine, white granite blocks, bear grass, and blueberries. I know every rock, every root, how the sun slants through the trees creating orange glowing puddles in the medium-brown duff. But today there isn't any sun. It's cloudy and everything above tree line is totally obscured in wet fog, and the wet pine needles clump up on my shoes.

I don't just know the rocks and roots. I know what has happened in this place and that. I can touch the trees with my fingers, trace the memories around in circles like the tree rings remember. This is where someone planted a memorial daffodil that blooms in the avalanche chute. Every spring I sit with it and look down into the valley, and think about his family.

This is where I found the line of club cards from a wallet that pinwheeled a thousand feet farther than its owner. I followed his library card and his gym membership, Starbucks card, CPR card, picking them up like bread crumbs on the icy face. Once I knew he was dead, I found his partner stuck on a small outcropping of frozen dirt. I told him I was sorry about his friend, and coaxed him down. He could have made it out on his own, but after watching his friend fall and then standing frozen there for so many hours, I think it can be tough to trust the first step. Sometimes it's just a confidence booster not to be alone.

This is where we stopped for a picnic lunch on Mother's Day, all wearing dresses, on our way to serve tea and cookies to all the hikers who came up that day. Eric, the guy whose sleeping bag I have, was wearing an orange and pink housecoat that zipped up the front, with a white pinafore collar. There. At that rock. Pure class.

This is also where Russell proposed to me during a lightning storm. We spent the night in the lookout at the top because Russ used to do maintenance on it for the Forest Service. In the lookout is a wooden footstool with glass feet. The lookout does have a lightning rod since it's the highest thing for miles, but the Forest Service suggests that during lightning storms, it is also prudent to stand on the stool for the duration of the storm. There is only one tiny stool, but we balanced on it for hours.

And this is where a woman with a broken leg told Russell and McCall that she much preferred piggybacking on McCall's back because his butt was bigger and therefore provided a much better shelf.

So this is Seattle Mountain Rescue. Occasionally I blush a little bit saying the words, "Mountain Rescue," since what we do isn't world-class. The Cascades are big enough to form a line dividing Washington State into two halves, and they are ancient and beautiful, but they're certainly not among the biggest, most impressive, or most famous mountain ranges of the world. Mostly we're just bushwhacking in heavy rain or groveling up slimy rocks with a few other people, looking like drowned rats. Which can be scary in its own way, but isn't like real, high-altitude, guts and glory, negative-40-degrees-Fahrenheit, legit mountain rescue.

And my friends and I, we aren't world-class athletes. We aren't bad, but we don't train all day—we work all day, and train at night. My friends have to take vacation days to rescue people. Or they leave after work one day, and spend all night lowering an injured climber or even just stuck hikers off one peak or another, and then they drive directly back and work the next day like nothing happened. The accidents here rarely even make even the local news. Many, many rescues are so small they are just the actions you would do for a friend who called you in the middle of the night, and we are just the people who are willing to get out of bed every third night and do them.

After only a couple minutes of hiking I run into an ESAR team, stopped on the side of the trail swapping gear around. They have the litter, which is like a backboard that comes apart in two pieces. A modified bicycle wheel attaches to the bottom, made for rolling people out. But I'm worried this equipment hasn't made it far enough up the trail yet.

We don't have a medic with us. SMR has medics and doctors, but today none of them responded to the call. We're only EMTs, and there isn't much we can do for a guy having a heart attack, if it even is a heart attack, which I have no way of telling. The gold standard of pre-hospital care for a heart attack would be to give morphine, oxygen, nitroglycerin, and aspirin, and not jostle him too much. But sometimes too much oxygen is actually bad, and I don't have that much anyway. EMT's can't give morphine and they don't have the right equipment to be able to tell what kind of heart attack he's having; if it's a right ventricular infarct, and I give him nitro, I could drop his pressure and kill him. But it's a moot point because I don't have any nitro, and neither, according to the 911 dispatcher, does he. Mostly we can just hand the guy four chewable baby aspirin, because that's the protocol for anyone with chest pain, and carry him gently but expeditiously toward definitive care. Our lot is more of a social skills thing, to convince a guy with agonizing, crushing chest pain to trust us by holding out baby aspirin.

As a rule the ESAR organization requires their teams to carry a lot of emergency gear, so they often aren't able to hike as fast as I can. I ask them who's the fastest person on their team, and can he go with me so we can each take half of the litter?

We start off with each of us carrying half the litter on our packs, but after another five minutes or so we stop again so I can take both halves because when I turn to look at my cohort, he's still upright, but he's gasping and looks like he's going to puke. "Russ, Bree." I call over the radio. "Can someone run back down and help me carry the litter up so it can get there faster?"

McCall is going to keep heading up, since he's an EMT too, and Russ and Taylor tell me they'll come down and grab it.

My mind tends to wander when I'm moving as fast as I can with a heavy pack. When I was pregnant with Vivi I was really sick, and afterward I wasn't as fast as before. Getting out skiing or climbing or hiking in the mountains together were always major tenets of my relationship with Russ. But after Vivi was born, he couldn't go out with me because he only has one speed, and I just wasn't fast enough to be a good partner. I tried everything to kick myself into gear, but sometimes when I'm out alone I have trouble motivating myself to train harder. Occasionally when I go out I find myself sitting on a rock with my eyes closed, just sitting there.

So when Vivi was really little, I used to hike with McCall once a week. He was a stay-at-home dad with two elementary school-age kids back then. My mother-in-law would come out to watch Vivi so I could get out of the house. We'd hike one thing or another, and it was great to have a conversation with another adult, work on losing baby weight, and regain some sanity. McCall came on a lot of rescues that happened during school hours, but now he's gone back to work, as some kind of tech manager for a tech firm.

After a few more minutes I see Russ and Taylor running down the trail ahead of me, and I throw down my pack and start fumbling with the buckles to release the litter halves. We're only halfway up. I toss Eric's sleeping bag out too, just in case they end up needing it. I hand them the litter halves, swing my pack back onto my shoulders and keep going up the trail as fast as I can while they attach the litter to their packs. Five more minutes go by before they catch up and pass me wordlessly, breathing hard, and disappear again.

The bear grass isn't blooming yet, but I can see the hard white beginnings that will be flowers in another few weeks. There is a lot of radio traffic. Eric says that Patrick and Bob are behind me, and I ask Patrick if he can take the bicycle wheel from the ESAR team when he passes them and run as fast as he can; he says he's already got it. Is already running.

I can do a lot of different jobs on rescues depending on who shows up and what roles need to be filled. On rescues where Caley shows up, he will typically come up with a plan and keep the overall operation running on the field side. If Caley doesn't show up, Russell will run it. If Russell isn't there, I'll run it. I go on more rescues than anyone else, so I end up running a lot of them. Anyone can do it, we just fall into old patterns. I guess it's a little autocratic, but it doesn't feel that way when it's happening. It just feels smooth. It doesn't take giving many directions, everybody's good at what they do, they want to be doing it, and they've enjoyed working together for ages.

Medical might be my default second job, but we've got lots of EMTs today, so I tell Russ I'll direct the carryout: make sure the litter keeps moving at top speed, tell the folks walking backward down the trail when to step over logs, when to turn, when to lift the man up over rocks, and when to unclip the wheel to pass the man under logs.

"Sure," says Russ.

The man is moaning, lying on the ground on a rocky shoulder near some little ponds. There is actually almost nothing that we can do. I help out McCall and Wes, check for a pulse but my fingers are so cold they're numb, take his blood pressure. Patrick shows up with the litter wheel, and we lift the man into the litter and balance it. I'm talking to him while we move him, telling him what we're doing. I'm not really sure what totally powerless people are supposed to say to someone who is dying.

"So," I say to the man, "this is a good crew. It's never a good day to have something like this happen, but the best crew was on call today, and you've got them."

It's true that we're on call every day, but I don't mention that, or that we're just volunteers.

"I want you to know, though, that it is a long way back down this mountain, and some people can die from situations like this. So if you want to live you have to focus on what you want to live for and not give up. That's your part. Promise me you'll do that, and I promise you we'll bring our A-game today too."

I look up, and Larry, Patrick, Wes, Russ, and Taylor are all listening. "Deal?" I ask.

The converted bicycle wheel supports much of the litter's weight, but this trail is miles of boulders and steep hairpin switchbacks, and the light is fading. In the beginning we tie a piece of webbing to the back of the litter for a tagline; four people hold the litter up and then a half-dozen other people grab onto this piece of webbing to keep the brakeless contraption from rocketing downhill with gravity. Nobody can see their feet, and this trail, like all trails, is too narrow to fit the litter in the middle with two people abreast on either side, so the people on the sides are intermittently mashed into trees, or have no footing and suddenly disappear downslope to be picked up at the next switchback, or are dragged through sticker bushes and have their feet run over. The folks on the front and back ends do not have a better time.

I'm jogging backward, in front of the litter, calling out rocks, letting everyone know when to turn, and holding an automated defibrillator, like the kind in shopping malls. It was donated a few years ago, and today someone scrounged it out of the back of the County's command van. I know the batteries on these things go dead, and they have to stay plugged in. I hope it was plugged in so it'll work if I need it. I have the litter moving as fast as I've ever seen an evacuation go. It's smooth and beautiful. Well, mostly. It's found a balance between smooth-ish and fast-ish. I can see Patrick's feet sliding as the litter pushes him downhill, he looks like he's skiing, but Patrick knows how to ski. I'm glad the man keeps moaning because it means he's still breathing. I ask each person taking turns on the head of the litter if they can keep talking to him. I'm looking for light banter, even if it's one-sided, but the guys are so gassed they don't have the breath to talk.

The evening's cold, but everyone is covered with a sheen of sweat, lifting the man in their arms over the rocks in the trail, sometimes passing him hand-to-hand down big drops and small streams without ever slowing down. There aren't a lot of us yet, so nobody gets a break and I can see the look of pain, the lactic acid built up. The guys start to straight-arm it, lifting with their backs once their arms won't flex, but nobody's lost their grip yet and I don't want to slow it down. I want them to run like I know they can, like perfection in motion, and there's more people coming to help. . . . They're just not here yet.

Out of the corner of my eye, I see Bob let go of the litter rail, not because his arm has given out, but so he doesn't take the litter with him as the dirt at the edge of the trail crumbles below his feet and he somersaults past me down a banked switchback of stacked boulders. The litter teeters for a second, and I jam my body into it; my hands slide along the bottom of the fiberglass shell, helping stop it while everyone pulls back together, feet slipping and stopping and slipping again. I've been shouting directions, but with the litter stopped it's suddenly silent.

"Bob, you okay?" I ask quietly with my back to the litter. I can tell the fall has hurt him. He lies in the bushes for a second, but we need him, so he gets up. He's lost his glasses, but it's almost impossible to see anything useful anyway, so he takes the rail back, says nothing, and we keep going.

Russ has spent this time on the radio trying to relay through Ed that we need the Fire Department to see if any of their medics would be able and available to hike up the trail to meet us. A medic rig had driven to the trailhead initially, but they're not equipped or trained to go into the wilderness, so they usually wait for us to meet them at the trailhead parking lot. Russ admits that it is a long way up Granite, but reminds them that now we were coming down. That we are already partway down. Finally they agree to hike up with an escort and meet us since the man is having some sort of cardiac event, and there isn't anything we can do about it. We have an AED and a bag valve mask and we could do CPR, if it came to that, but the thing is that we've never successfully done CPR on anyone balanced on top of a modified bicycle wheel and carried by four people down any kind of steep trail. When we do CPR, we have to stop, take the wheel off, and lay the litter on the ground, and that means that we can be stuck there for a long time.

Finally, one of the medics makes it up to us. The other one is still behind, hiking as fast as his lungs will let him. We stop, still holding the litter, and cut the man's shirt off so the medic can get a twelve-lead and defib patches on his chest and hook him up to the monitor that ESAR carried up for them, where we figure out it isn't a heart attack, but unstable tachycardia, a heart rate fast enough that his heart doesn't have time to fill with oxygenated blood between contractions, which means that that oxygenated blood isn't getting pushed through his circulatory system, and the circulatory system includes arteries that feed oxygen to the heart, and if the heart doesn't get enough oxygen, just like with a heart attack where one of those arteries gets blocked so no oxygen gets through, heart tissue starts to die and it hurts. The medic tries a few times, but can't get an IV in, and he says he wants to try to cardiovert: use a medium amount of electricity to shock the man's heart into a better rhythm.

The medic mutters under his breath, "I don't want to dick around any longer with pain meds. We need to do this right now." He looks over at me, "Do we need to set the litter on the ground or is it okay for everyone's hands to be on it?"

I spend a tenth of a second thinking about aluminum's conductivity. Yup. It's conductive. But if I decide to take the wheel off, it'll take five minutes to get it off and then put it back on again.

All my friends look up at me very seriously.

I figure that it's unlikely he's really touching the rail, since we've got a pad under him and he's mostly in a sleeping bag. People always get bent out of shape about these things.

"Go for it," I tell the medic. No one else says anything, and it's suddenly very quiet.

We're making just a little pool of bluish headlamp light in the dark. McCall is holding the monitor and I've got all the paraphernalia from the IV attempts in both hands, so neither of us is holding the litter. Both of us are standing a little bit behind the medic, where he can't see us, but everyone holding onto the litter can.

The medic leans over the man and says, "Sorry, man, this is going to hurt like an f-ing mother," and then he dials it up, and says "All clear." My friends are not all clear, but the irony of this statement is lost on the medic. The medic is busy.

Larry is standing across from us, holding onto the aluminum litter rail, and together McCall and I smile at him with wide evil smiles while he glares at us, and then the medic pushes the shock button. The man's whole body launches vertically, and he screams once, a release of air and agony. He crashes down again and a second later, when we're all looking at the monitor, the man suddenly clears his throat and says, "Wow, that's so much better." But the medic looks at the monitor again and says "Yeah, so I'm still not happy. We're going to do this one more time." And he bumps the dial up 50 joules.

Neither McCall nor I look at Larry. Larry won't make eye contact with me, and gives no hint of whether that was painful or not. He didn't let go of the rail the first time though, and I figure that's good enough to keep going with this plan.

The medic hits the button again.

We stumble into the parking lot five minutes before midnight. Which is two hours and fifty-five minutes too late to pick up Vivi from my mom and still have it count as same-day pick-up, since we have all agreed that 9 p.m. is a reasonable time for my parents to finally lock the door and go to bed. It has been far more than four hours.

We help load the man into the medic's rig and it takes off, along with some of our clothes and Eric's four-hundred-dollar sleeping bag. It's too late to get dinner anywhere, which means catching up with McCall will have to wait until another day.

Everyone's leaving. I'm ready to go home, but I have to do some paperwork first, filling out forms by headlamp leaning up against someone's warm truck hood in the parking lot.

I didn't know the man, which was surprising. We'll never meet again. I think that if I were a professional I wouldn't give this day another thought. The man did not have an unusual problem. We didn't come up with an unusual solution either; this happens every day. Mundane. Memorable like water on a duck's back. Like rain in the mountains. Like wind in the meadow. Russell will be asleep seconds after climbing into bed and won't want to talk. Everyone moves on and there is just a rocky spot next to some small ponds added to my mental lexicon.

But it's a lot of effort and bruises to move on without savoring victory. I want to claim some small part in saving someone's life. When I get home I sit on my sofa in my retro house, eat some victory Grape Nuts and feel happy. In the morning, I'll go pick up Vivi.

RATTLESNAKE LEDGE

EIGHT DAYS BEFORE CHRISTMAS I try running Teneriffe, a foot-hill next to and sort of akin to Mount Si off Exit 34 in North Bend; Teneriffe is slightly longer and steeper. But there is so much snow I finally give up. It's untracked waist-deep powder above the waterfall, and I can't make the top and back in time to pick up Vivian from her playdate. And I shouldn't have worn trail-runners. My ankles are getting cold.

I feel a certain weariness. Maybe it's loneliness, although I don't usually mind being alone. My bones hurt. It's hard to be tired because I never know what else is going to happen in a day. How fast I'm going to need to turn it around. How wet to let my gear get. How much to let my knees hurt because I might sleep through the night, or I might have to go out again in five hours, or five minutes. Maybe it's just tiring, willing the next call not to happen until I get the power back, until some time that's sort of convenient and I have my shit together. But I like it, too. Just knowing that I might have to go back out any minute makes me appreciate being dry so much more.

It starts raining in the afternoon. Two hours after I get back from Teneriffe, my phone beeps. There's a rescue: two guys calling for help somewhere around Rattlesnake Ledge, one exit up I-90 before Teneriffe, and on the other side of the freeway. It's still raining. Not the hardest rain I've ever seen, but close.

A gated road runs along the parking lot for visitors to Rattlesnake Lake. Watershed Protection, employees of the City who maintain security for Seattle's main supply of drinking water usually unlock the gate for us during rescues since the parking lot is almost always full. We drive down the access road to a grassy field next to the trailhead. But this time, the parking lot is not full. It is utterly desolate except for the car the two guys drove. I see the car as I turn in, a black hulk darker than the dirt of the lot, reflecting my headlights for a second before the windshield wipers cut the moment.

The guy from the watershed unlocked the gate for us anyway, to save us the five-minute walk. The field next to the trailhead is full of mud, covered with rain, and I'm afraid that my car will high-center in ruts I can't see in the deep grass.

Deputy Josh, filling in for Ed who has the night off, is on the phone in his SUV, and Allen, from another rescue group that drives tricked-out trucks, quads, and snowmobiles up old logging roads, is pulled up next to him. Nobody else is here yet. There are no logging roads to drive tonight, so Allen is staying in the parking lot, answering the radio and doing paperwork. I'm wearing mountaineering boots, which I almost never do. I usually wear trail-runners everywhere, but my shoes are still wet and my toes are cold.

I pull my umbrella out of the back seat of the car and stand outside Josh's window for a while, but it looks like his phone call isn't going to end anytime soon.

Allen has his window rolled down. "Hey, Bree," he says.

"Hey, Allen," I say back.

We have a pretty good relationship, withstanding even the last time he gave me a ride on the back of his snowmobile. Allen is a big enough guy that I can't get my arms all the way around him, and I can't quite fit on the seat behind him. I was hanging onto his jacket pockets for dear life, crouched over the rear track. It added to the exhilaration of the speed and the noise. I usually just ski, even though it takes longer, but sometimes we don't have that kind of time.

"What's the deal, Allen?" I ask.

"Two guys went hiking and one of them fell over and hit his head," says Allen. "He thinks he's going to die, so he's refusing to hike out— it just sounds like someone needs to hike up there and march him back down here."

The rain is hitting my umbrella so violently that it's hard to hold.

"Okay, head injury of one sort or another," I say. "I'm Team 1. I'm going to start up."

I pack my first-aid kit, a C-collar in case he's more significantly hurt, extra band-aids in case he isn't, and a bunch of extra clothes, plus a twenty-dollar reusable emergency blanket, and start over toward the trailhead.

This is a trail, but it's a trail at its most urban, only four miles round-trip. Most of the people who come here are not hikers. They are picnic-goers who swim in the lake in the summertime and then stroll up to the ledge; groups of girls in spandex with cell phones in their cleavage; and couples taking wedding photos. People come here for their first hike after they've resolved to lose the weight, or to hold hands while looking down at the lights in the valley down below and make out with their lovers. Many people have not yet figured out that it's not appropriate to throw plastic water bottles off the ledge, and consequently it does not look like wilderness.

Three ledges overlook the valley, and it's a fair drop from the first one, so people also sometimes come to die here. They land in almost the same spot every time, in amongst generations of plastic water bottles and Frisbees and golf balls, disintegrating foam footballs, a toilet seat and plunger, and the informational signboard that used to be at the top. Walking through the garbage in the dark at the base of the ledges, along the slimy black rock and rotting soccer balls, looking for a person while the blood is still wet always comes, for me, with a visceral repulsion of these woods-cum-dumping-ground, mixed with thankfulness that we can at least make sure people won't ever be left here.

One morning, when I had a summer job working for Watershed Protection, we found that some person or persons had nailed together over a dozen man-sized crosses made of pressure-treated 4x4s, carried them up to the overlook and then just left them wedged upright with a chalk note that read, "Philippians 4:13." I looked up Philippians 4:13. It says, "I can do all things through Christ which strengthens me." If I could do all things, this is not the thing that I would have chosen to do. But that's me.

The crosses were heavy, which I suppose was the point. I spent the rest of that day dragging them back down the trail again with a maxi pad taped onto the side of my neck and the crosspiece on my shoulder. I found a salamander on the trail that day, too. I have a picture of myself bearing both a cross on my back and the dusty orange critter in my palm. Or maybe it was a newt. I'm not great at animal identification.

Rattlesnake Ledge has a nice view, but right now I'm not sure why anyone would choose to hike to this place on this rainy night. I know I'm not too keen on hiking it. Stiff boots suck to hike in. I find it more like clumping than hiking. I hate when I can't feel the ground under my feet, and boots make my knees hurt. I have my trekking poles in one hand, and my favorite umbrella—the one with multicolored polka dots—in the other, trying to embody the urban-wilderness interface at its best as I drag up the trail by myself. It is raining so hard that I would get instantly soaked without the umbrella, and I don't know how long this rescue might take.

After a mile and a half, slush balls are falling from the sky. They're not really tree bombs but slush clumps falling directly from the sky. My umbrella shudders under the weight of the blows, its slender stalk threatening failure, and the wind starts picking up. I resort to holding the umbrella out in front of my head like a shield.

Base calls to say that they've clarified the nature of the rescue, and it is actually two people stuck over the edge of the overlook in two totally separate spots. One of them fell to his current location and has a head injury.

This is not good news.

It's my job to rescue people, no matter what has just happened to them, but—and this sounds whiny—I can only carry so much on my back. If someone is stuck over the side of a cliff, I have a kit for that, but someone has to mention that fact so I can grab that gear. Right now I have the large first-aid kit instead. I hate it when this happens. It's so unprofessional, and it never seems to happen to anyone else. I'm not upset with Allen, I should have talked to the deputy directly.

I am muttering loudly to myself while the folks in base try to figure out what to send up next when finally the wind becomes too much, and with a loud snap my umbrella collapses like the freezing, slush-covered, nylon slap in the face it is.

Sometimes the urban-wilderness interface is more wilderness, and sometimes that means underprepared people get fucked, whiny or not. I'm not sure how many times I'm going to have to learn this.

My phone starts ringing. It's Garth, one of the usual suspects willing to show up on a weeknight to help retrieve some hikers stranded over the edge of a 250-foot cliff in inclement weather. I asked him to pick up SMR-2, the more reliable of our two trucks. The North Bend public utilities department has been allowing us to store it in a back corner of their property, where it grows moss like a giant chia pet, but we're grateful for the space. Before this, Eastside Fire let us store it at one of their stations for a little while, but nobody is really psyched to house someone else's truck for free, so eventually they asked us to move it out. If we lose the public utilities spot, then we're in trouble.

"I found the gate combo, but the truck is missing," says Garth. I turn my back to the wind and think for a minute, and we both remember at the same time that there is already another mission going on. Larry has taken SMR-2 with the snowmobile trailer up to Tonga Ridge to get some guys stuck with a bunch of kids and three dogs in the middle of nowhere.

"Well, okay," says Garth with false joviality. "I'll just go get the SMR-1 then. Is it still in the back of the North Bend Forest Service back lot, or have they kicked us out yet?"

SMR-1 is actually in better shape than it has been in years. When McCall mentioned to the last Vehicle Chair, Art the suspender-wearing curmudgeon, that the power steering in the truck had gone out, the response was, "What are you, a pussy?" It wasn't in jest. But Art was just reassigned to managing the newsletter, and there was just a truck work party, and the truck got an oil change and new tires. We threw out 250 pounds of equipment older than we were, and retired some group gear onto our members' mantlepieces, like the hinged cast-iron crampons with the Scottish straps, the spray-painted orange pulaskis that we used for ice axes sometimes when we'd forgotten ours, and a bunch of first-generation pale-blue avalanche beacons with earphone jacks but no earphones. Those didn't go on anyone's mantelpiece— we just threw them out.

The truck also houses everything we really care about, all our meticulously cared-for ropes and rigging kits, the avi rescue bags, climbing gear, personal flotation devices, medical kits, and dog rescue kits, the main things of value that Seattle Mountain Rescue owns, sitting in labeled boxes in the rear of the truck on stylish shag carpet.

This gear, the life-safety equipment we actually use, comes from donations. Most people who donate money to SMR are families of climbers whose bodies we recover. Almost no one we rescue alive donates money. I guess maybe folks feel that if we pulled it off, then our stuff works well enough. There might be some legitimacy in that. It takes more human capital than financial, anyhow. SMR is an all-volunteer nonprofit with a chairman and a board of directors. We have about sixty climbers total, and we're all on call every day of our lives, and as volunteers we do, on average, 135 rescues a year. We also do the admin, run the training program, keep up our continuing education, maintain our accreditation with the Mountain Rescue Association, do the fundraising, and speak to school groups, outdoor clubs, and anyone else who asks. Plus we research and order our rigging and extrication gear, and then carefully wash the mud off it and hang it to dry after rescues.

In the past five years, we've had a 45 percent increase in the number of rescues. I think it keeps our focus on rescuing people, but right now we're about as lean as an organization can be. It can be hard to throw a fundraiser when whatever night you pick, you know there will be a call, and half the organizers will run for the door.

Someday, though, I know we're going to get it together to launch a capital fundraising campaign for a building. We need a building so bad it hurts. It sucks trying to dry out 1,200 feet of rope with a space heater and a dehumidifier in the back of a truck that looks like a chia pet. It makes the shag carpet smell like the '70s. I wasn't alive in the '70s, but I assume smelling like the '70s means BO and carefree wet dog. It also sucks to be constantly trying to find free meeting space big enough to do medical trainings or get the crew up to speed on using new equipment, or to have our board meetings. It sucks not having a home.

Sixty-eight years of rescuing people with two trucks and a post office box. I can only imagine how cheap property must have been in North Bend in 1948.

"Be right there," says Garth. "Two minutes. Two minutes. . . ." and he hangs up.

I should have brought ski goggles. The rain is turning to painful sleet. I'm starting to accumulate an exoskeleton of ice. I turn back into the wind and keep walking through the slush.

Garth's calling me again. "You remember the combo?" he asks.

"For the Forest Service gate?" I asked.

"No, I got in the gate, the combo for the truck to get the key out of the lock box."

"Try S-M-R," I say.

"It's numbers, not letters," says Garth. "Never mind, I'll look it up on the SMR website. What's the password to get into the members section?"

We are a classy operation. "You got this, buddy. I believe in you," I tell Garth. Unbridled laughter comes through the phone, and he hangs up.

I hear over the radio that the second team, an ESAR team, is just leaving the trailhead.

There are three major ledges, but Ledge One is the first and biggest. As I get close I can hear a man screaming into the wind.

Would it have killed me to bring a rope? Team 2 has a rope, two miles down the trail. Fuck. There's only so much stuff I can carry. But it wouldn't have killed me just to throw it in. And my helmet. And my harness and some anchor material. But no woman is an island. At least I can get there, assess the situation, take charge, and see if I can scream some calming words until someone else shows up.

As I round the corner a dark human-esque shape about twenty feet away hurtles itself toward me but then falls, sprawling out on the rocks at the top of the ledge. I continue walking over.

A crack runs the length of Ledge One. It's only maybe two and a half feet across, but it's thirty feet deep, and the developing ice storm has coated the rock's surface with a half inch of black ice. All the bushes on my side are coated with ice and already bent under the weight of it.

The man—as is now apparent—stopped yelling when he fell. I can see that he's picking himself up, and I keep walking over. He's wearing a grey sweatshirt with the sleeves balled up around his hands. His leeward side is soaked and his windward side is shiny with dark, thickening ice. I want him to bend his windward arm at the elbow to see what will happen.

"What happened?" I ask. It turns out, not so much.

"My buddy and I just jumped over to the other side of the crack to go look over the edge of the cliff," he says, "and it was just raining, but then it got all icy, like, super fast. I didn't want to slide down into the crack or slide off the edge of the cliff trying to get back, so I said we should call for help."

"Okay," I say, nodding.

"Then my buddy said whatever, he could jump it, but his shoes slid out from under him and he disappeared down over the edge of the cliff. He hit his head, but it's fine, he landed on a little ledge."

"How do you know this?" I ask.

"Yell real loud and you can hear him," he says.

"Alright, I'll try that. Strong work," I tell the man. "Take your sweatshirt off, here's a jacket." I take off my pack, dig past the C-collar and the first-aid kit and pull out the first jacket I come to, which is my red SMR one. It's a soft-shell but will stay dry for at least a bit, and it's wind-resistant. I hand it over. "So, you called 911 over an hour ago; what made you decide to jump the distance right when I got here?" I ask him.

"Well," he says, shrugging, "I just saw you coming and I was like, what the hell?"

"Go stand back from the edge under that tree," I tell him. "Where exactly is your buddy?"

I pull out my ice walkers. I used to think that only old people shoveling sidewalks used ice walkers. I used to think that there should be no space between managing terrain with running shoes and needing boots and crampons. Maybe I am getting old. But a person could break a hip if they fell over on this ice and then it would hurt for, like, three seconds before they slid over the edge of the cliff and died.

I've picked up a half-dozen bodies from the bottom of Ledge One. Some people fall off. A lot of people jump. Extrapolating from others' tragedies, I know exactly what I would look like when I landed. But it's clearly not crampon terrain. It's a really benign place most of the time. Shoot. Half the time when I run up here, couples in loafers and high heels stand at this exact spot having their wedding photos taken. It just slopes down toward the edge a little bit. Not that much sloping, but enough.

I move cautiously forward and peer over the edge. The second guy is only twenty feet away, roughly six feet down on the next ledge, which also gently slopes downward. There's a big rock right at the edge and he's sitting with his feet braced up against it. His pants are blowing up his legs with the wind. What is it about people not wearing socks? Maybe he's wearing the anklet kind. Are socks with running shoes a fashion faux pas for men? I'm not sure. I'll ask Garth later.

"I'm coming down, don't move," I yell down at him.

"Not moving," he yells back.

He does not move. I climb gingerly down. He is similarly iced; each individual leg hair glistens in the beam of my headlamp. At least, they intermittently glisten because I think my headlamp might have a loose connection and it keeps turning on and off.

I brace my butt against the rock, wedge my pack against the rock so it doesn't blow away, and we put on all the gloves, hats, and jackets I have in there, and then I dig down to my twenty-dollar reusable emergency blanket. It's been in my pack for almost a year. I picked this one because it came in a vacuum-sealed package—very low profile. I don't really want to open the package because it'll never pack this small again, but it could be more than a few minutes before Garth and the crew show up. I think, what the hell, right? I give him my now mostly empty backpack to sit on, and tuck the emergency blanket around him.

"Your buddy says hi," I tell him. "Can you tell me what happened? Do you know where you are? Do you know what day of the week it is? Are you having any pain anywhere?" It's like twenty questions. Nothing sounds immediately life-threatening, and I can't see any blood on his head. My hands are pretty frozen so there's only so much I can do beyond just talking. He seems basically fine. Once I run out of medical questions we talk about movies for half an hour. He likes action thrillers. I like documentaries about global warming. We talk about action thrillers.

Team 2 shows up and Garth is all, "We thought he was over the real cliff!" and I'm all, "But it's icy. You try climbing back up without ice walkers." Garth laughs like he's sympathetic that I'm an old woman.

They belay Nick down, and we put the patient harness from SMR-1 on the man with no socks, it looks very professional, and then Garth pulls him back up the ice steps. It takes five minutes.

Back at the top, the first guy has taken off with my jacket. I radio down to whichever team is hiking him out to get it back before he goes home. I stuff the emergency blanket into my pack and it fills the entire space.

We didn't use much rope, which is good. Garth will stick it back in SMR-1 and turn the heater on. It should be dry before Christmas.

RED MOUNTAIN

THE SUMMIT OF RED MOUNTAIN is a narrow northwest–southeast-running ridge. Narrow enough that you can stand with one foot on each side. On the east, facing the Middle Fork of the Snoqualmie River, the tiny summit drops off into a 600-foot cliff.

The storms here usually come in from the west. Every winter the wind blows the snow into giant cornices, sagging mushrooms that hang over the southeast cliff edge, blurring the point where the rock ends and the undercut snow hanging over air begins. Every year these cornices form and grow and sag and fall and form again with the next storm cycle.

Now, on the first Wednesday in February, twelve inches of new snow has fallen over the weekend but the weather is clear at 3:45 in the afternoon. The King County Sheriff's Office called because someone found skis and a backpack at the top of Red Mountain. But no skier.

It's still clear out, but the day is already losing light and a front is forecast to come in with a significant temperature inversion beginning at five. Rain is expected to start by ten. The Northwest Avalanche Center reports avalanche conditions in the area as moderate, but the snowpack will become more dangerous as the inversion warms the snow, and everything will be *significantly* more dangerous as soon as the late rain starts.

Ryan was once a part of SMR, but we lost touch long ago. Now we're just acquaintances. I know a few facts about his life. He has a master's in philosophy. He works construction, wears vests, has six-inch unkempt reddish-white hair that waves in the air and matches his perpetual sunburn. He has a broken-down truck and a dog. He's married now; his wife wore the most beautiful wedding dress I've ever seen, at least it looked that way on Facebook. And he can ski like something from a fable. We did the Ski to Sea together, a relay race that links Mount Baker in the North Cascades to the ocean near Bellingham. He skied, and I did the canoe leg down the Skagit River with Aaron, a long time before Aaron graduated from medical school and moved to Portland and jumped over the waterfall and then relocated to Africa.

I'd never canoed before, and Aaron said he'd take me to practice once before the race, in the Snoqualmie River near my house. The day we picked was pouring rain, and the river was on the verge of flooding. It was a cold day, maybe 40 degrees by midmorning when we put in. Aaron looked confident. He's a pretty big guy, skinny but tall with reddish hair, and he laughs loudly and frequently, and he always looks confident.

My neighbor Peter wanted to come, too. Peter is a naturopathic doctor. Carnation is thirty miles east of Seattle, a town small enough to not really support a doctor of any sort, especially a naturopath, so he has a lot of time off. He and Aaron wanted to talk about determinism—whether or not people have free will—and he said he knew how to canoe, so the three of us got into the canoe with Peter in the middle. Peter's oldest daughter agreed to watch Vivian until we got back.

Within two minutes on the river we hit a tiny rapid and flipped over; then we got caught in a whirlpool and spent a freezing half hour in full raingear, going around and around in tight circles before Peter, who turned out to be a better swimmer than a canoeist, dragged us, and then our canoe back out. The whole time, a couple with their dog stood on the bank yelling down to ask us if we wanted them to call the fire department, and I kept yelling, no, we were fine, thanks. When we crawled out on the bank, Aaron just laughed and I shook my head and smiled. Aaron and Peter continued their conversation about whether this was a stupid decision, or just our fate, and we walked back home to get dry clothes while I wheeled the canoe behind me.

Twenty-four hours later at the same whirlpool, a couple was throwing a stick for their dog until it jumped in and got caught. The dog's owner leapt into the water to try to save the dog. He got stuck in the whirlpool, too, and began to struggle. Then the man's pregnant wife jumped in to save the man and the dog, but she also got stuck, all of them spinning like clothes in a washing machine.

A policeman called 911 to report the family in trouble. He told the dispatcher that he wasn't a strong swimmer, so now he was standing on the far shore, watching and holding a throw bag.

Someone called the fire department and Darby—whom I didn't meet until much later, years after the whirlpool disappeared and the river moved and moved again over more seasons, and he joined SMR—told me that when he got there with the rest of the firemen, the dog had managed to swim to shore, the man had drowned, and Darby could tell the pregnant woman was going down for the last time. So he jumped in before his crew even knew where he went.

Darby managed to grab the woman and get them both into an eddy, but then he realized that they were headed downstream very quickly while he was doing everything he could just to hold the woman's head above water. The bank at this spot was all steep levies covered with half-frozen blackberry bushes. The policeman ran down through the tangle, tossed his throw bag and pulled Darby and the woman to shore, thereby saving her.

Darby has a tattoo left over from an earlier phase of his life that says, "Fuck the Police." The same policeman came to his aid again just a few months later in another water rescue, and Darby told me that it was an unexpected thing to come to love a policeman so much.

Darby told me this story a few years after the whirlpool incident, while we were driving the sixteen rough miles of dirt road and wash-outs up the Middle Fork of the Snoqualmie River to recover a body on Mount Garfield.

"That's a good story," I said, "but it's odd to realize that our paths so narrowly avoided crossing before."

"Maybe fate dictates that people only meet in certain times and certain places?" suggested Darby. But I don't really believe in fate. Soft determinism, tops.

Aaron, Ryan, the rest of the crew, and I did finish the Ski to Sea, but technically we were disqualified because it turned out that the canoe we borrowed was only fit for use as a flower planter box, absorbing so much water over the course of the paddle that we were unable to lift it out of the water unassisted at the end of the leg. I'm not strictly sure, though, if that was because it was too heavy, or because we were laughing so hard.

Ski to Sea aside, I didn't usually get out with Ryan's crew back then. Ryan and his girlfriend at the time, Monika, and their friend Oyvind and a small group of guys from Everett Mountain Rescue were skiers together initially, and their strength and power on snow was a beautiful thing. I would see them on Mount Baker every once in a while as they passed me skiing up and down the mountain.

The closest I actually came to keeping up with that crew on skis was one Mother's Day on Mount St. Helens, the volcano between Seattle and Portland that blew up in the '80s. I'd invited EMRU to join SMR for the cherished skiing event where hundreds of dress-clad backcountry skiers from all over the Pacific Northwest honor their mothers by taking silly pictures of themselves along the crater rim at the top. I have a picture of all of us standing together looking sunburnt and happy. Monika wore a pink tank top and matching skirt, and Oyvind had something rayon, knee-length, with a large floral print. I couldn't keep up with them that day either, but I did have a great satin bridesmaid's dress with so many layers of tulle that the A-line skirt floated out in a beautiful, giant circle. It was cool enough that I didn't care if I had to keep clamping in my elbows so the dress didn't slide off.

A year or two went by. We got older, skied, and climbed a lot. Got more wrinkles and age spots, learned some things and forgot others, made some friends and lost others, and the mountains basically stayed the same. The summit of Red Mountain, in particular, stayed the same.

So now on that first Wednesday in February, I'm driving up Snoqualmie Pass into the midafternoon twilight to see about the missing person who left skis and a backpack on top of Red Mountain above a 600-foot cliff. A few minutes later, I get a text saying that the skier was Ryan's girlfriend, Monika. She'd headed out alone for a powder day and hadn't come back. But what good is it to know who it is ahead of time?

I should spend this time—driving 90 miles an hour up Snoqualmie Pass, my little car shuddering—finding the right words to say to Ryan. Something communicating empathy, but yet not implying that I have any idea what this really means for him. I know that nothing is going to be the right thing to say.

I also feel a need to come up with a plan that can fix this, but at the same time I know there's nothing I can do that is really going to fix anything. All any of us can do is show up so that Ryan's not alone.

It takes me almost an hour to get from my house to the pass: a lot of time to figure out nothing. I suppose a professional would use this time to mentally inventory equipment, to review safety procedures and strategize. I know this, but I'm a volunteer. I listen to KEXP and carry a plastic glow-in-the-dark Madonna in my glove box, and I don't have enough information to come up with a strategy beyond avoiding preconceptions. I feel too old and too young, and like I'm just going to keep on holding the steering wheel, and figure out the rest as it comes.

In the parking lot at Alpental there's a lot of slushy snow, and it's totally dark. The county sheriff's Command RV sits in the middle of the lot with the floodlights on, illuminating wet snow starting to fall in impossibly large flakes. The light illuminates Ryan standing behind the truck next to a garbage can, crying.

I still don't have a plan. I'm not a hugger. I've always wished I were a hugger, but I'm not. It feels like forcing myself into someone's personal space, instigating an exclusive therapy grief circle that I don't have license to be a part of. I feel like I can never really touch someone else's trouble, and the act of trying seems like propagating an illusion. The physical embodiment of a platitude. Maybe I overthink it. But now I'm naïve, and I try it anyway. I walk over and try hugging Ryan because I don't have anything to say, and because there are people walking around everywhere but nobody is paying him any attention. Or, more likely, everybody can plainly see him standing there, but nobody knows how to interact.

It goes about how I thought it would. He's shaking hard enough that it's contagious, launching me backward like any two objects with corresponding polarity will, and I keep moving away. I don't know how to do this.

Ryan called Oyvind first, even though Oyvind is in Everett Mountain Rescue—this isn't his jurisdiction—because Oyvind is one of Monika's main ski partners and because he's a great skier. I can't fault Ryan for calling his best friends first. Oyvind showed up a few minutes after I did.

KCSO had known abut this incident since early afternoon, but they'd held off calling SMR for a while while they tried flying their helicopter over Red Mountain, thinking they could locate Monika while it was still light, before the weather moved in. The pilot reported that a cornice was lying in the basin, and it looked like it had started a small loose slide that ran 400 feet farther down. But they couldn't see the cornice fracture line, or any sign of Monika in the basin below.

Then they called SMR. And now it's dark.

While Russell, Garth, the rest of the crew, and I put our packs together, shoveling gear around and buckling our boots, Ryan says he thinks maybe she could have hung up somewhere on the face of the cliff. Or maybe she got caught in the slide and is under the tree line where the helicopter can't see. Maybe she is still alive.

I think 600 feet is a long way to fall. The cliff is a vertical, massive dark wall on the backside of a mountain rising up from the Middle Fork. But I also know better than to judge what is survivable.

Years ago, I worked as a climbing ranger at Mount Rainier. During the off season my team leader Charlie and his climbing partner Gabe got caught in an avalanche and fell 3,100 feet down Mount Deltaform in the Canadian Rockies. Gabe lost his pack, his hat, and his gloves, and lay exposed and utterly broken on the glacier for three days and nights before a Royal Canadian Mounted Police helicopter spotted him. And he lived. He said later that it was because Charlie had come over and told him that he was going to walk out for help. Gabe knew help was coming, and that gave him the strength to stay alive. The RCMP found Charlie's body a few feet from where Gabe had been, and it was obvious he'd died in the fall. But I know this is a thing that happens, surviving the unsurvivable. I know better than to say anything either way.

Ryan is a better skier and a better climber than I am, and we both know that if Monika is still alive, he can get there faster. But tonight, Ed the SAR deputy won't let Ryan leave the parking lot because this is a suspected fatality, and the basin is a crime scene, and Ryan's the victim's boyfriend.

I know I look like a shit-show, digging through SMR-1 and coming up with a bunch of pins, a few ancient screws and old tools and random bits of rack, with a vague notion that it might be somewhat technical trying to get around the mountain to the southeast side. I brought skis, but left my ice climbing stuff in the laundry room. Stupid.

I dump everything in my pack and walk back over to Ryan, careful to stop four feet away.

"I'll do a good job," I say. "If she is alive, I will find her. I will find her no matter what, and I will do a good job, because this is the thing that I know how to do better than anything in the whole world."

"I need to go with you," says Ryan.

And then Russell, Garth, Oyvind, and I ski away, and Ryan watches us leave, still standing next to the garbage can.

This part is familiar. I've been skiing after Russ for most of my life, before and after I married him, and Garth and I have gone out together hundreds of times—any time he can get away from Kidz-bounce, his warehouse of bouncy castles for birthday parties and drop-ins, or updating his guidebook to Exit 38, the closest major climbing area to Seattle. I don't know how many rescues we've done together. Hundreds.

This time, though, I feel like an interloper. Like this one shouldn't really be our job, that my crew has been foisted on a situation that should be resolved by Monika's friends, because it would be fitting that they bring Monika back and we should let them do it as a professional courtesy. I imagine that might be what she would want. If I were orchestrating today, if I were in charge of fate, I would run interference so her friends could take care of her. But then . . . I don't have that power. And also, I don't know Monika more than in passing, and I don't actually know Ryan or Oyvind that well either, or know what they would want. I'm not sure that getting Monika's body back any way from Sunday is what Ryan wants at all.

And then we're just going through the night and my lungs are burning, but I will keep up the pace. Big fat flakes fall through the light from my headlamp and make large fuzzy shadows on the snow between my skis, and the steam from my breath makes lazy curling tendrils somewhere far behind me, and the flakes and the shadows blur the lines ahead of me, and to each side all is soft, silent blackness.

I think there is an idea that people will take unreasonable risks to try to rescue someone they know. Later, many days after this day, there will be a big storm on Mount Rainier. I'll be feeding my neighbor Jenn's dog Banjo while she climbs the mountain. Jenn's also in SMR and she's one of my best friends, so I feed her dog. But she won't come back from Rainier when she's supposed to. Then she'll miss the first day of her new job as a children's librarian. The Park Rangers will call out all the area teams from the Mountain Rescue Association for help, and everybody will come.

Oyvind'll end up in charge of the Everett Mountain Rescue folks, and I'll be the point person for the SMR crew. With the weather still nuking, Oyvind and I will have a conversation in the Emergency Operations Center in Longmire just before we ski out and start looking for Jenn, and he'll question whether I understand the line that I can't cross because if I do keep going, trying to save my friend when the weather or conditions are too dangerous—if I go against all my training and experience and common sense, and die, too—that would piss everyone off.

After a small kerfuffle, though, Oyvind is going to have to admit that I'm right: even if I leave my friend to die, and survive this day, a little bit of who I am as a person is going to die, anyway.

Oyvind says later: "But this proves my point. How is it even a good idea to put yourself in a position to make that decision, if there's no decision you can pick that you can live with?"

I'll just shrug and turn away because I think it's some combination of fate and love that brings me here. One I don't even believe in, and the other I won't change. And we'll have that conversation, that day, because of what's happening right now on this night, searching for Monika.

Because we come to the top of a wind-loaded chute between two rock walls. On our way up here, the snow has been mostly light and unconsolidated from the previous few days, well bonded to the older snow below, but this is a narrow, dark thing on a new lee aspect, and steeper—we can't see the bottom. And it's much warmer than it was. There are some exposed rocks on the ridge, and we can see water running down the rocks in tiny steady streams, trickling into the snowpack, making it heavier and heavier. Even the fat snowflakes have stopped. The four of us stand for a minute on the ridge and take turns lying on our stomachs, peering down over the edge.

We don't have team leaders in SMR. No one makes a go/no go decision that we all abide by. I appreciate that no one's making these decisions for me. I know better than anyone what I can do and what I can't, and if I do something wrong, I want it to be me that decided to do it.

We stand on the ridge, talking about the conditions. We talk about Monika. We talk about other options, contingency plans, backup teams. We talk a lot about the weather, and we talk fast. Oyvind says he thinks the chute will hold for another few hours, and he's going to go down even if it's by himself. Garth said he doesn't think it will hold, so he's going to stay on the ridge. Plus, his staying here will help us because we're going to lose communication with Ed and the Command RV as soon as we drop down the backside, and we need someone to maintain our comms. Specifically, Garth says, if the chute slides and we die, he'll call it in.

"Thanks, Garth," I say.

"Any time," says Garth.

Garth has a daughter in middle school. His ex-wife married Doug Caley, another lifetime SMR member, so now he and Caley share custody of Ellie. Once Ellie broke her hand while her mom was out of town, so Garth and Caley both rushed her to the ER where the staff assumed that they were a gay couple. After initially being confused, the guys decided to play it up, to Ellie's great amusement. They're great dads. I think Garth might be thinking about Ellie when he says he's going to stay.

"I think it looks fine. I'm going down it," says Russ. Usually he says his piece and then commences enacting his plan while other people are still talking.

But I think about the line.

Oyvind thinks it is an acceptable risk. Possibly if he goes down into the basin, and it doesn't slide, he could save his best friend's life if she's critically injured down there. Oyvind has a fishing business, but he teaches avalanche classes on the side, and in his best judgment, with all the ways we can judge conditions from here, he doesn't think it'll go. And, I assume, if it does and he dies, his wife would take care of his three kids.

But my situation is so far removed from his. Would Oyvind do it if he were going down with his baby's momma? Russell and I share a preschooler with big blue eyes and blond pigtails that stick up in the air, who is asleep at Grandma's right now, spooning a pink polka-dot security blanket. She would miss us if we died together in an avalanche. She would grow up and say that we didn't love her enough to stay. Threw our lives with her away for someone who was already dead, someone who had made her own choice to ski in the mountains and accept the risk that comes with that, someone who only needed us for one day, for one reason, when we knew Vivi was going to need us every day, in a million different ways.

I have a love-hate relationship with backcountry skiing. With alpine rock climbing it's so often easier to tell when things are going bad. Usually, a series of more painful issues tip you off. Hunger or cold or exhaustion, choking back sobs of terror, being sick, dealing with injuries, rushing to compensate for going too slow, or futzing with equipment—this kind of thing comes first, until the culmination of many issues finally becomes overwhelming. I'm not saying it always happens like that, but it frequently does. With avalanches, though, instability doesn't kick you in the gut to tell you it's there. You have to look for it. It doesn't touch you until it takes you out. Damn avalanches.

So now I'm looking at it. But working through dangerous terrain and difficult situations and eventually, somehow, getting to the person to help them, this is what I do. If I don't, then who am I? But I can't help acknowledging that it's a given that Russ should be here, forever the man of the hour, able to fulfill his obligation to his family with his life insurance policy. My internal dialogue, keyed into societal norms, narrates, "But should his wife have come too? She's risking turning their child into an emotionally shattered orphan, and that's on her."

I don't have any less experience, or skill, or training, but I sense that if I die trying to rescue somebody, folks will blame it on tunnel vision. That I couldn't see the big picture, didn't think about the consequences for Vivi. That I'm a bad mother for gambling with my ability to be there for my child every time she needs me for the rest of her days. But if I don't go, I'm telling my daughter that moms aren't a good choice when you really need to get shit done, because women with young children at home will always think about family first—stuck on the big picture, not able to stay focused on the task at hand. I'll be telling her that women are too conservative, aren't committed enough to be good at the work. It's a catch-22. Why am I more worried about what people will think of me than about the snowpack? I wonder. "Because protecting your reputation matters as much to your future as protecting your ass. What people think of you has real consequences," says my internal monologue, "don't mess anything up."

I can't—wouldn't—tell Russ not to go. We don't tell each other what to do in the mountains; nobody in SMR does, and of course he needs to be here. All the guys do. Somehow it's a given, even if Garth stays on the ridge, somehow it's more okay for him to do that. But maybe it's just my own skewed perspective. But from what I can see, the only choices I actually have are to go too, and pull it off, or else back away and admit that I shouldn't be here, that I should go home and vacuum something. Psych. It's not a choice. I have to go, and it has nothing to do with my risk assessment which, adding up everyone's mental state, the likelihood Monika's still alive, the temperature inversion, the darkness, and the wind-loaded chute, tells me to stay on the ridge until it slides in a few hours when the rain really starts, and then go down.

At the annual Northwest Snow and Avalanche Workshop, they always talk about decision making. How people don't stop to think about what they're doing. But I'm suddenly struck by the realization that it's even worse to know that I have carefully evaluated the situation and all the information, and come up with the plan that I think is right for me, and then deliberately decided to do something else.

It goes beyond just needing to care less about how other people see me. I need to figure out how to make the fact that I'm a mom not affect the jobs I'm entrusted with. The key is figuring out how to get there. That seems harder than getting down into the basin.

"Base, Team 1," I call over the radio, and then go on to explain what we're going to do.

Garth sits down on his pack behind our pile of skis. The wind is starting to pick up with the approaching front, and to do a radio relay he has to stay fully exposed on the top of the ridge. He pulls out an emergency blanket, tucks it gently around his ski boots, turns his headlamp off, and hunches over, hugging his knees with his radio on his lap. It's almost midnight.

The chute is too steep and narrow for us to ski. We leave our skis at the top and go down it one at a time. I make Oyvind go first and then I ease down, moving from one foot to the other, my headlamp illuminating my ski boots and then blackness below. Even though I've dug people out of avalanches days after they died, weeks later, months later, I still can't picture myself being dead as the result of one as well as I can picture success. Maybe we never really can understand risk clearly, decide clearly, until we have experienced both.

There is no moon.

"Hey, Garth, we found the bottom and we're still in one piece," I radio up.

"Yeah, well look at that!" says Garth cheerily. "So base says the rain is definitely going to start at 6 a.m. now, so you might want to keep that in mind for getting back out again."

"Okay," I radio up. "We're going to yell after three. One, two—"

I release the mike key and scream Monika's name.

"And again, after three," I say, "one, two—"

But when we listen, there's only silence. Silence, and us squinting out into the darkness, focusing on the crazy way the snow sparkles at our feet.

Perspective is so hard to get with a tiny headlamp. I can tell there is avalanche debris in the middle of the basin. We're walking awkwardly through it in our ski boots. I go up to the base of the rock at the bottom of the cliff, and find a crater four feet deep where the cornice landed and triggered a loose snow avalanche that ran down the basin below it. I can't see how far it went. Farther than my light reaches.

We start doing a beacon search and using the RECCO, a handheld detector that helps locate the tiny reflectors some manufacturers sew into skiing outerwear, but we get no signal. Monika was skiing alone. Why wear a beacon, skiing alone? So that if you die, it's easier for people to find your body? Who thinks about that when they head out in the morning? I can't fault her. It's a morbid thought.

Turning around and stumbling back down frozen chunks of debris, I find a stretchy cloth headband with flowers on it.

"Hey," I yell, "I found a stretchy cloth headband with flowers on it."

"Yeah," says Oyvind, "she just got it last week. She really likes it."

I put it back down on the snow where I found it and spot-probe around it, although my flimsy aluminum probe is no match for the ice chunks. I can feel it bending one way and then another, its angle untrue. When I'm finished I keep the probe extended, carrying it like a vaulting pole, and I start making my way downhill again.

I find a glove lying on the snow. I pick it up to make sure Monika isn't lying under the snow at my feet with her hand still in it. I see a boot liner, and lift that too, and then set it back down. We walk the entire perimeter of the avalanche debris, finding no footprints leading out.

The toe of the slide turns out to be about 400 feet below the cornice's initial impact. I walk a long way before I finally get close enough to see the cornice itself. It's the size of a VW bus. There is blood spattered in the snow at its base. We spot-probe the shit out the whole area, and find nothing.

The next thing we would normally do is to use flags to mark the border of the slide, the clues we found, and the areas we've searched. Do organized probe lines, with everyone standing in a row, moving one step forward, shoulder to shoulder, probing right, left, and center. We'd document everything with photographs and sketches. But right now, none of that is going to happen because we are standing under the line of still-hanging cornices, minus the one, and when it starts to rain, they're going to fall.

Aaron from the canoeing incident and a few other guys from SMR have found a way around the other side of Red Mountain, and at about one in the morning they join us in the basin.

"Hey, Aaron," I ask, "can we go back out the way you guys came in?"

"It was terrible!" yells Aaron into the almost total silence. "We can go back up it, but cheese and rice! It would be insane!"

Aaron is always really happy, even when he's talking about how much he does not want to do something. He's also prone to yelling, "Whatever! It's fine! Just do it!" when something is not fine. It is a tell that we should not do that thing, and he does not want to do that thing, whatever it is. Our pattern is that I suggest that we could go some other way, and he agrees, and then we go some other way.

Aaron is a much bolder climber than I am, but we're pretty evenly matched for technical ability. If Aaron says his route was bad, that means it must be scary as hell. The chute we came down will only be in progressively worse shape as the night wears on. The only other way out that we can think of is possibly down Goat Creek to the Middle Fork.

For Ryan's birthday one year, a group of sixteen of us skied up Mount Snoqualmie, just west of Red Mountain, for a three-hour tour. It was really foggy, and we drank too much whiskey with our birthday cupcakes at the top, and just about everybody skied off the wrong side—the north side—of the mountain. Because it was just a social trip, nobody was really paying attention and we didn't realize the error until we were just above the Middle Fork of the Snoqualmie River, 4,200 feet down.

We could have gotten out that way; a road runs down that valley to the town of North Bend, but it's fifteen miles of rough potholes and washouts that isn't plowed in the winter. That day we laughed a little bit, and then turned around, and booted back up to the top of Mount Snoqualmie, and skied back to Alpental, figuring it would be faster than booting the whole way down the road and hitchhiking back up to the pass. So we did the entire Snoqualmie Middle Fork descent tour by accident. The last half of it was mostly slide-slipping down bulletproof ice by headlamp in the middle of the night, but the rest of the whiskey made it all okay. But now, from where we are, it's too dangerous to boot back up; we need to continue down from this basin and navigate toward the Middle Fork Road, the way we accidentally went before.

Now I'm standing here, shivering in the basin on the backside of Red Mountain, and I think, having touched everything, seen it, that

Monika is dead. I promised Ryan that I would find her and bring her out no matter what. But I can't find her, and I'll have to deal with the emotional and strategic consequences of that failure later. For now, my attention is starting to refocus on taking care of Oyvind. It's three hours before dawn and the rain is starting, spluttering at first, but already the chute is a crazy, sagging thing. Aaron and the rest of the crew need to leave—Aaron has an exam for med school, and everyone else has to be at work in a few hours.

Oyvind wants to stay and look up at the cliff in daylight, to make sure that she isn't hung up on the face above us, obscured by darkness. He wants to make sure that there's no way she's somehow gone over a succession of small cliffs below the basin, and he wants better photographs before the headband, glove, boot liner, and the edges of the slide are snowed over. The front is coming in warm, but we know it isn't going to end that way, and all the clues will be lost in fresh snow.

I don't have anywhere else that I have to be right now. I'm still not gainfully employed, and Vivi is with her grandma. I have the time to work the Middle Fork route out. Nathan (a joint SMR-EMRU member) who came up with Aaron, says he'll stay, too. Russ will take over for Garth as radio relay at the top of the saddle, because Garth is mostly frozen and needs to get to Kidzbounce to set up for a birthday party. Aaron, Garth, and the others say they'll carry all our skis out and leave them in the parking lot at Alpental. And then they leave. Oyvind, Nathan, and I watch their lights climbing, with our beacons in our hands and our probes out.

There is a little rise in the middle of the basin with a grove of trees. We pick the biggest tree and shovel out a small bench under it because we think it could be marginally drier under the branches, and then we all sit down shoulder to shoulder and wait for daylight. I'm wearing this pumpkin-colored synthetic parka that I bought after I got lost on the Muir Snowfield in a storm for four days and nights without a tent back before everyone had GPS. After seeing what the Pacific Northwest did to my down jacket and sleeping bag—basically soaking and then refreezing them into a single congealed shape with the weight and consistency of frozen turkey—I bought this jacket. With it, being cold and soaked to the skin is still kind of miserable, but not really too bad. I'm not scared of freezing, and I can accept the rainy darkness like another old friend in the tree-well huddle.

Oyvind actually falls asleep for a few minutes. I'm thinking about nothing, and then I can suddenly tell that it's gotten light enough to see. Nathan and I realize together that we're just staring at Oyvind. There's really nothing to say. I think the goal's just to be here so that somebody is here. I climb out of my sixty-four-gallon industrial trash bag that I always carry as an emergency winter bivy. It works really well for slushy conditions. I can tell that the clouds are higher, thicker. It's still raining steadily. Those cornices are going to fall.

I look up at the cliff now that I can see it, and there's only rock, no sign of Monika. It's time to leave. Even Oyvind has to know it, but I can tell that he doesn't want to give up. He keeps scanning the cliff face.

As the temperature warms, we sink deeper into the snow, waist-deep in places. Looking at the map, it's about two more miles from the basin, following the creek out, to the Middle Fork Road. This is the scenic middle section of a nice ski tour; it would go faster if we had our skis.

I'm not sure how much snow will be on the road when we get there. I figure we're going to have to post-hole some of it, but hopefully not all fifteen miles. Trying to make progress while sinking so deeply into the snow with each step is exhausting. I call Russ on the radio to see if they can send some guys from the 4x4 unit to drive their trucks in as far up the road as they can to meet us, and he says he'll ask.

After we drop down out of the basin, we spend a long time searching the small cliffs down below it, which are also covered with avalanche debris. The snow is now consistently crotch-deep with some deeper spots, and booting downhill is slow going. Oyvind is thorough in a way that you hope your friends would be, and Nathan and I tell him to take all the time he needs. We do transceiver search after transceiver search, and we yell, our voices echoing back to us.

Once we drop down into the Middle Fork our radios can't reach Russell anymore. Before we lost contact with him, I asked if he could relay to base that we thought we'd be at the road at nine. But radio relays are like playing Telephone, and the message that the 4x4 team eventually gets is that they should go get brunch and then try driving their trucks up the road later in the day. And then we lost contact with everyone and couldn't straighten the message out. When we finally get to the road, though, we do realize that nobody's here to meet us.

We can't find the bridge, get tired of walking the bank looking for it, and finally ford the river, not swimming, but close. We can't get any wetter, so it doesn't matter. And then we walk down the road. At first, it's slushy snow-covered, then later slush-covered, and later still just rocks. The rain is hard enough to kick up mud between the rocks, and we walk in silence for a long, long time.

The 4x4 guy is very apologetic when he finally shows up some hours later. He's a big guy who says he runs on the warm side. His defrost can't keep up with three soaking people, and he has to open the windows, but he lets us keep the heat cranking even though I can see the sweat pouring down his face.

"You don't happen to have any food in here?" asks Nathan. "Any bars or cookies or breath mints or anything?"

"Oh," says the 4x4 guy. "If I'd known you'd be hungry I would have gotten you guys some take-out from brunch."

After a while the silence starts to get awkward, so he follows it up with, "I have a secret stash of Little Debbie snack cakes under the back seat."

We fish those out and eat them, and then Oyvind falls asleep again.

It's Thursday morning. Thursday afternoons, I volunteer for Vivian's co-op preschool. I get home, take a shower, get Vivian back from her grandma's, and pack up banana bread that I thankfully baked the morning before. I also slice whole bananas into rounds, just scoring the skins because the kids like peeling them themselves, and pack a Tupperware full of Dixie cups with six chocolate chips each. Then Vivi and I head out again.

I don't mind being snack mom. I can handle setting out the carpet squares for story time, and mixing bleach solutions, and supervising the play-dough table, even when it gets frenetic. But what I really like is pushing the kids on the tire swing. I put three girls on the swing and twirl it far, far faster than they've ever gone before. The tiny girls giggle and scream with their hair flying straight out. I get to see the first time they're confident that they can hold on tight enough to see themselves through. I get to see what could be their first taste of the crazy joy that comes with pushing the limits of safety and decorum to see what's really possible.

I did get an evil look from the preschool teacher one time when Emma threw up all over Maddie. It's true, I wanted to tell her, life is dangerous when it's being lived.

Friday, it rains in Carnation and dumps snow in the mountains.

Vivian and I go to the Woodland Park Zoo, because they have an indoor play area with a three-story tree house that looks like a giant banyan tree. It's awesome because Vivian, her backpack, and I can all fit up the ladders and down the slide at the same time. She likes it when I climb up behind her, and she feels the need to take the backpack with her stuffed seal and pink polka-dot blanket everywhere because she's always concerned that she'll suddenly get dropped off at Grandma's, and I won't be back in time to pick her up before bedtime.

The weather's still bad. There's no precipitation forecast for Saturday morning, but a large weather front is predicted to move in Saturday night and nuke everything again into Sunday. SMR's plan is to wait twenty-four hours after the Sunday storm cycle, and look for Monika again on Tuesday.

But unbeknownst to us, KCSO sent a Backcountry Avalanche Rescue K9 team, also known as the BARK guys, back into the basin during the small weather window on Saturday morning, because Ed decided he didn't want to wait until Tuesday. Ed didn't tell us, he just called around until he found a group willing to search earlier. But then, we didn't get the job done the first time, and Ed likes people who get the job done.

After setting these plans up and sending in BARK, Ed took off work on Saturday. So it was Pete, another deputy, who was in the Alpental parking lot waiting for the K9 team to finish searching when he found out that Ryan and Oyvind had snuck into the backcountry with the BARK crew. Now they were in the basin without permission. Since there was still an issue with Ryan being the boyfriend of a dead woman in an open death investigation, and Oyvind was freelancing—not an emergency worker in King County, and not specifically asked to be here—the sheriff's office couldn't tolerate it.

Pete called BARK on the radio and told Ryan and Oyvind that he would have them arrested if they didn't return to the parking lot immediately. But they refused, telling Pete that they had to keep searching, and he could arrest them later. Pete can't access that kind of terrain without a helicopter, and the weather was too bad to fly, so he called Russell and told him that they weren't actually going to need SMR to search on Tuesday, because they were actually searching now with BARK instead, but he did need SMR to field a team to go to Red Mountain right now, to bring Ryan and Oyvind out so he could arrest them. He wanted us on the road immediately.

Russell and I are sitting on the sofa when we get this call. In one breath, it hurts that Ryan and Oyvind didn't tell us they were going to search again, but I understand why they didn't. It hurts, too, that Ed and Pete didn't tell us that there was a new plan, and it didn't involve us—if for no other reason than we could've quit organizing, and let our guys know to reschedule their week. But I don't think, even if Ed had asked us, that we would have tried pulling off searching again Saturday morning, because even if we did find Monika, we knew we wouldn't have time to get her out before the second predicted storm rolled in. I haven't worked with BARK much, but I know by reputation that they're totally awesome. Maybe, psychologically, I just find it hard to fail.

I'm worried for Ryan and Oyvind, because they're in an impossible situation. They're going to lose, no matter what happens. Russ and I don't say any of that. Russ isn't much for talking about feelings.

"I'm not going to do . . . that," he says, gesturing in a vaguely circular motion, which I take to mean he isn't going to drive up to the pass and ski in to tell our grieving buddies that they're going to have to stop searching for Monika because they have to come with us and get arrested.

"No," I say, "but if we don't agree to do it, Pete is going to find someone who actually will do it."

"You go," says Russ. "Vivian and I are going to stay here." And he plops our squirming child on his lap, grabs the remote, and turns on *Phineas and Ferb.* End of conversation.

I know Vivian's not old enough to watch *Phineas and Ferb.* The cartoon mummies will give her nightmares. "Only look at the platypus," I tell her.

Okay, I think to myself. I can run interference. I can tell Pete I'll go get them, and I will do it. I can ski in immediately, and ski out with them, but only when they're done. I'll give them space to do what they need to do. Maybe if I do this, it will keep anyone from being arrested.

My gear is finally mostly dry, hanging off every door and cabinet in the house. I've put my pack together so many times that the gear falls in by itself, like it does for Mickey in *Fantasia*. Grooves are worn in the glove box of my car where my skis' tips rub; they slide down at an angle, wedged along Vivian's car seat in the back.

SMR-2 is now housed in the lot behind Eastside Fire Department's mechanical shop in Issaquah, surrounded by the blackened hulks of cars the fire department has cut up with the Jaws of Life and then burned for live fire practice. I drive to Issaquah to pick it up even though it isn't strictly on my way. Jessica comes with me—she's the only one I called who didn't turn me down when I explained what I was looking for.

As soon as we get to Alpental, Pete jumps out of his police SUV and tells me he's just heard on the radio that Ryan found Monika. Pete is upset—grateful that Monika is found, but upset that Ryan found her. I feel relieved on both counts.

It turns out that BARK only finds buried avalanche victims; they aren't prepared to carry anyone out. Pete doesn't want Ryan and Oyvind to touch her, let alone move her. He wants me to go in and document the scene before anybody disturbs anything. Ryan and Oyvind don't have any equipment, and aren't prepared to do the recovery anyway. I think they must be fried, so I doubt they'd try it.

"You can take it from here, right, Bree?" asks Pete.

"I can do that," I tell him.

I need my crew, and it's already one in the afternoon. It'll be dark at four, and the storm front is coming in. Pete will send out a text message to all of SMR. And Tacoma. And Everett asking for more help for the recovery. He seems to have forgotten about Ryan and Oyvind.

Jessica and I grab as much gear out of the truck as we can possibly carry and start skiing in. By the time we get back up the shoulder on the side of Red Mountain, Russ and Caley catch up with us. I don't ask Russ who's watching Vivian.

I don't know Jessica that well. We've skied some of the volcanoes together, and done some cragging in Index and Leavenworth. We shared one avalanche mission on Granite Mountain, where a guy was completely buried, but with a sizable air pocket around his face and his hand. He was able to breathe, and somehow managed to get his fingers to his cell phone in his breast pocket, and dial 911 by feel. He'd been buried there for hours before we got there and dug him out. Anyway, recovering Monika with me wasn't Jessica's first mission, but it wasn't more than her fifth, either.

I've known Caley since I was fifteen. After he and his first wife divorced he rented a room from Russell in a condo that Russell had barely finished remodeling. Russ just wanted to be alone, surrounded by perfection, but Caley wanted the spare bedroom, and a bunch of the rest of us with sketchier living situations came over all the time to cook and take showers in between climbing trips. Russell had created a lovely guest bath.

After he moved out of Russell's, I rented a room from Caley and another SMR guy. I used to walk to the mailbox, and they would come driving up behind me, yelling, "There's a rescue, we threw your pack in the car, get in!" I learned to keep my pack packed, and to wear running shoes everywhere. Eventually this bachelor pad plus one fell apart. Caley married Garth's ex-wife, and I married Russell.

Recently, Caley helped me graduate from high school. I was volunteering for the fire department in Carnation because, ironically, the first step toward getting hired with a fire department is to volunteer for years—the more years, the better. But I also started applying for fire-fighting jobs. I applied for one with the City of Kent and I made it through most of the hiring process. The oral board went well. I thought it was a good sign when the head of the panel said, "Your husband is a fire fighter, isn't he? You have a good coach." But then the clerk called to tell me that being a fire fighter requires a high school diploma. I was homeschooled, and started college when I was thirteen; somehow, I never got an actual high school diploma. But this job required one, just proving that my bachelor's in philosophy, which everyone said was going to be entirely useless, is in fact entirely useless. I can't help feeling my life is going in the wrong direction. I've always felt self-conscious for not getting a master's, all my friends have at least one, but now I'm headed back to high school. Fantastic. The City of Kent gave me a week to graduate.

My friend Jenn printed a very classy, perfectly legal, home-school-based high school certificate off the internet for me. Thank goodness for librarians. All I needed was for someone to sign their name attesting that I had fulfilled the graduation requirements that had been outlined in my hippie-dippy, only-existed-on-paper curriculum.

I couldn't think of anyone better than Caley to sign it. He had taught me so many educational things during my formative years; he taught me how to "fake it till you make it," and how to write a two-page official report devoid of any content. He did sign my certificate, although with some trepidation. I made him shake my hand, too. I have a picture, because I thought I should document this major life milestone. I didn't get the job, but it wasn't for lack of the proper educational credential. Anyway, Caley and I have known each other for a while.

We're finally skiing up the shoulder of Red Mountain to get Monika, when we run into Oyvind, Ryan, and the BARK crew heading out. It's early dusk. The sky is that pinkish gray where there's enough light to tell that the sun is setting, but the clouds are thickening again, and the next storm is bearing down. They ski past me, and we say nothing of consequence to each other because nobody can think of anything to say. I know better than to think I have anything to say. Saying any-thing is inserting myself into a place where I have no business. Some-times there is only the action. Like making a casserole. If I vary the steps or the ingredients, then I have no idea how it's going to turn out.

We don't talk to each other either, Russell and Caley and I, but not because we don't have anything to say; it's because we already know what the other person is going to say, so talking is redundant. We all know what to do.

As we start heading down, Jessica says, "Hey! What's the plan for this whole operation?"

"Oh, right," says Caley, and starts explaining.

We leave our skis at the top of the saddle again. The chute slid at some point since Thursday morning, and now it's all avalanche debris at the bottom. The BARK guys actually skied down it after it slid, but I don't need the thrill. Looking down, I suspect it would be more like free falling while pointing your skis right and then left. Plus bodies can be unwieldy enough to carry; I don't need to carry my skis back up too.

By the time we get down into the basin it's fully dark, snowing thick and fast. The snow is so deep at the bottom that it comes to our waists, wet like mashed potatoes and just as heavy. We are soaked from the fog above the snow and the water in the snow, and the kind of darkness that soaks into your bones.

We find Monika where they moved her, to the bench in the grove of trees where we spent part of that first night. We don't search for where they found her. We don't look for anything because it's snowing so hard, everything is covered over, and we need to keep moving. It'll snow another foot or more tonight.

When we lift her, we sink down and find no bottom for purchase, so I have to build anchors across the basin with a picket and a rope, and pull her body behind me.

We have a 300-foot static line with us so we can raise her, but when we get to the chute we realize that it won't reach the top. There's no easy way to build an anchor halfway. The chute is almost vertical, and the snow isn't the kind that makes it easy to build a secure anchor, especially since we would need to space-haul off this anchor with a pulley and a ratchet, raising her body by leaning backward with all our weight, counterpointing her weight with ours. Our pickets wouldn't hold.

I stand in the basin with Jessica, looking up while Caley and Russell slowly climb with the end of the rope. When the rope runs out, they tie all the webbing from the rigging kit together, and then the cordelettes—thin cord reserved for building anchors—from their harnesses, and then their slings and prusiks, any bits of climbing gear strong enough to pull. Just as they run out of things to tie together, they manage to reach the top of the saddle. While they pull from the top with one incredibly short reset after another, Jessica and I balance precariously under Monika's body, and push up on her feet.

Eventually, once we make it back up the chute, and just as we're starting back down the shoulder, Everett Mountain Rescue arrives to help us. More people from Ski Patrol and ESAR show up, and we all carry her out together.

When we get back to Alpental it's three in the morning, still dark and still snowing. Tired people stand all over the lot. I lose Caley, Russ, and Jessica somewhere in the crowd while folks are leaving. On the one hand, I don't think we need to say anything to each other, we all just need to go home and get a couple hours of sleep. But at the same time, sometimes I wish we did say something.

It's almost five before I finish the paperwork and drive back, alternating between using the defrost while shivering violently, and turning on the heat while peering out the fogged windshield. I fill the gas tank and park SMR-2 next to a car that, thanks to the Jaws of Life, has just become a convertible, its roof lying upside down next to it, filling with water like a kid's wading pool.

But I can't get out of the driver's seat. It's freezing outside, dark and silent, raining, but it isn't the cold that keeps me here. I'm not sure what to do next, how to bear witness to someone else's story when that story intercepts mine. What do I do as an emergency worker? What do I do as a friend? If this is a job, then I do my best to create a space to make sure the people in the story can do what they need to do, and then I step back to let them grieve with their support network. Anything more would be intrusive. And as part of their community? I would do the same thing, I suppose. Maybe make a casserole.

By eight I'll be home, making waffles and doing laundry for Vivi and Russell, and that's okay because I have to keep going. But part of me just wants to hold the weight of this day, this series of days, because it is more important than the laundry or the search for a way to make money. Death is supposed to connect people, and I find that I'm hugging the steering column with my face pressed against the wheel like the baby monkey in a documentary on attachment disorder that I watched once in school, and all I want is to be held, and not feel alone.

A few days later, they had a memorial ski for Monika on Red Mountain. I know because I saw the pictures on Facebook. I hope they brought whiskey, and skied off the right side of the mountain.

I ask Vivian to go for a walk with me. She wears her ladybug boots and carries her monogramed yellow umbrella. She wanted to know why I didn't bring an umbrella, too, since it's still pouring rain.

I say, "Because the rain is the only continuous thing between the two disparate worlds I live in, and it's an awkward transition back and forth." I say, "I want my worlds to bridge together at least at one point, and this is the only common factor I know."

I think for another minute and say, "I want to be involved and to hurt, to know I'm human. I want to be connected to other people. I want to be vested in this world and do the kind of work that you do for someone you love."

Vivi says, "I want an orange kitten with white spots."

"Yeah" I say, smiling and reaching for her hand. "I hope we get what we want. Until then, let's walk."

CHAIR PEAK

IT'S THEIR DAY OFF, THE two men who leave the parking lot at Alpental to climb Chair Peak. A lovely day for a moderate climb, and conditions are good. The ice isn't fat, but it's present, which is good for Western Washington. They've come to stretch their legs and swing their tools up a few pitches in the winter sunshine, to talk about the future, stand quietly together, confident and easy at the top. The day is so cold that sweat stings as it evaporates, and breathing hurts like mouthwash: they are refreshed. It's a good day.

I'm spending the day volunteering for the fire department. Vivian is growing up fast, she's got one more year before she starts kindergarten, and Russ says I need to have a job locked in by then—he's not going to work all day while I sit around, watching daytime TV while she's away at school. So every night after they go to bed, I stay up applying for all sorts of jobs. I think fire fighter might work for me. Fire fighters only work eight days a month, so I could still be here for Vivi when she gets out of school most days, and I could still volunteer for SMR. And fire fighters get to deal with chaos from time to time, but they don't have to worry about paying for gas to fill up the fire truck before they deal with it.

The trouble is that I'm not seeing the bonding at the fire department like what happens with my crew in the woods. I don't think a lot of these guys even like each other, and the culture is hard for me to handle. I don't want to listen to "The Men's Room" on KISW all day. The other night during drill they made a middle-aged volunteer, who doesn't want a job, who just wants to help people, crawl around on his knees and bark like a dog because they thought it would be funny. I know hazing is a tradition and traditions exist because they help groups feel unified, but all I feel is alienated. They tell me that they'll lay off, but only if I can prove that I'm worth helping. I think, maybe it's just this particular crew. Or this station. Or this department, and once I put my time in here, I can find another one, and that one will be what I'm looking for. Or maybe the problem is me—I'm just not a good-enough cultural fit, and I have to be willing to change.

When SMR gets a new volunteer, we invest. If we approve their application, they've proven everything they have to prove. We pay for classes, give them a mentor, drag them out for sufferfests and sandwich sharing in the North Cascades. We arrange beer nights, cajole them into joining us at the climbing gym and doing laps with us week after week. We tell them how happy we are that they're here with us—there aren't really a lot of climbers who can, and want to, commit the time. Every time we get someone new, we're grateful.

At the fire station, I ask my lieutenant for advice on how to navigate the culture. He tells me, "The right to respect has to be earned." He tells me the key is to be humble. To be able to understand how little you actually understand, to be willing to start at the bottom and work hard. In the morning, we go to the local senior center, and my lieutenant teaches me how to do blood-pressure checks. A pretty basic skill I've used consistently for twenty years. I don't mention that, though, and when I get it right the first time they think they've taught me well. And I think, really, they do have a lot to teach me, it's just that I'd rather focus on power tools and throwing ladders. We stay through the center's seated Zumba class, and then later, with today's lesson done and four more hours left in my shift, I clean the kitchen back at the station, wipe crumbs off the countertops, and try to stay out of the way for the afternoon.

In Carnation, the fire station is staffed 24/7 by three rotating shifts of paid fire fighters, but altogether the station runs fewer calls a year than SMR does. Also, most of the fire department's calls last only a few minutes. There aren't actually very many fires. In the past year, there hasn't been much more than malfunctioning automatic fire alarms, burn ban violators, and EMS calls. Most of the time the fire fighters just show up for medical emergencies, and then call a private ambulance company, like the one I used to work for, to actually transport the person to the hospital. An EMT working for a private ambulance company makes far less money than a fire fighter though, little enough that I've eliminated going back to that as a career option. Plus I've gotten used to SMR's cadence, where an average call lasts six hours, and it's not uncommon for a single rescue to last for three or four days; and there are no shifts, I get called out for everything.

Seeing how other emergency workers approach the job has made me realize that I like the camaraderie of spending long hours battling chaos in bad weather, year in and year out. I've thought about what would happen if I got paid to do SAR; I used to when I was a park ranger, even longer ago than my ambulance driver years, but I like helping people for free. I think that in the backcountry this service should be a gift, freely given by our own user group. Climbers helping climbers. Somehow, I can't help feeling like it's worth more, service freely given, even though it's hard to explain how something can be worth anything if no money exchanges hands. I guess it's been so long now that I can't think about doing it for any reason besides love.

And I like everything about doing SAR, except feeling second-rate since I'm not a professional. I'm not a professional because I don't get paid. Not getting paid makes people think I suck. I wish there were a way to be a professional, and not get paid.

I stand in the bay doors and look up at the sky. It's a clear afternoon, and cold, and I can picture myself out climbing, free, my crampons squeaking in perfect névé. I can smell ice, metal, and chaos, and it makes my fingers twitch; there wasn't much chaos in Zumba class today.

A few hours later, the two climbers are descending Chair Peak, down the rappel gully on the ridge's southeast side when they trigger the avalanche. Avi conditions for the day were listed as moderate, but it had been windy, and wind loading in the gully had formed an isolated wind slab, sitting on an earlier rain crust about thirty centimeters down. One of the climbers said later that he remembered triggering the slab after downclimbing only a few feet, saying that the slab was so well consolidated that at first he did not notice he was moving. But then he realized that he was.

At the fire station, my shift of being respectfully enthusiastic while cleaning stuff finally ends. I've just bought a new car, a Honda Fit. I love this car. I saw it, and I had to have it. I put a roof rack on it for carrying skis, bikes, and kayaks. I run my hand along the roof rack with affection before climbing in.

My longest kayak is twenty-two feet long—much longer than the car—so I needed to tie it down front and back. The only way to do this is to use a giant eyebolt, the kind that comes in the spare-tire kit, and screw it into the bumper. But my spare-tire kit contained only one giant eye-bolt and I needed two so that I could tie down both ends of my boat. I called the dealership to order another one. They put me on hold.

After fifteen minutes, the man on the other end, his voice strangely cracking, like he was choking back sobs, said, "Ma'am, if your car ends up in a ditch, the tow truck will only need to pull you out in one direction. You don't need two of them."

I have to wonder, now, if this guy thought I was incompetent because I'm a woman, or if I'm just being overly sensitive—like a woman. All I know for sure is that I will get along better in this world if I can come off sounding less like a volunteer, less like a woman, less like a mom, too. I need to sound more competent to the average observer. And yet, I care about being able to help people for free; care about doing it like a woman, like a mother. It's crazy how much I want to hold onto who I am, even though I know these labels are hurting me.

When it stopped, after the avalanche and the terrain tried to rip him apart, the climber was buried. But his friend managed to dig him out fast, even without avi gear.

If I close my eyes, I can see that. The focus and strength it took. I know what his breathing sounded like as he dug toward the climber, because I've moved my hands down through the snow, clawing blocks out of the way, and listened to my own breath. And the climber lived. Even still partially immobilized in the snow, he was conscious and aware that his throat was full of ice. I can picture him retching and then lying there for a minute next to his friend, just breathing.

Leaving the fire station, I push in the clutch and will the gear to catch. Driving a stick is one of those basic life skills that I somehow missed out on, and it always comes up. I hate being incompetent. So I bought this tiny, lima-bean-shaped hatchback to force competency.

It takes me three minutes to drive home from the fire station. While I'm getting out of the car, a text comes through: "Two people caught in an avalanche on Chair Peak." My first reaction: I'm more anxious about shifting back out of first gear than I am about this rescue. Maybe it's because the clear day has turned into a clear night; I'm guessing that a helicopter will be able to reach these guys, and all I'll do is drive an hour from Carnation up Snoqualmie Pass only to turn around and drive back down again. That means I won't get dinner made for Russ, or catch up on work for Vivi's co-op preschool. I'm on the board. My job this week is to purchase some kind of lid for the sandbox, so neighborhood cats quit shitting in it. The parent educator from Bellevue College says being on a real board like this is a great opportunity to get leadership experience and practice working with other people, but all I feel is ennui. Plus, Vivian will be disappointed because I promised her I would play Chutes and Ladders, and instead she'll spend the evening in her room, stuck there until it's clean; but she won't clean it—she'll be beading or something, humming to herself on the floor in a semicircle of Beanie Babies, and no one else will ever know that I gave up this evening, showed up at the pass and offered to help with this rescue. But I go. I turn the key, put the car in reverse, and ease off the clutch while pressing the gas, willing it not to jerk in uncontrollable engine death throes and die.

Not going is risky. The only way to guarantee that someone gets to the climbers is to climb to them. Helicopters can be really hit-and-miss, depending on the location and weather. The weather here is often suddenly bad.

Snohomish County, one county to the north of us, has a SAR helicopter program that runs on donations. Their fundraising slogan is, "Support the Last Resort." I'm not sure what to call those of us who still do rescues in bad weather, climbing, hiking, or skiing in and carrying people out when the helicopters can't fly. "Support the Really Last Resort?"

When I get to the parking lot at Alpental a smattering of folks are already there, mostly 4x4 guys sitting in their trucks with their light bars flashing, and one other SMR guy named Drew who plays electric guitar, and has perfectly white hair, brilliant blue glasses, and nicer skis than mine. The deputy sticks his head out of the King County Sheriff's Office's Command RV and says, "Thanks for coming, guys. Y'all can head home."

I don't know him. He's not part of the usual rotation of deputies I work with. He's probably never done an SAR before. He says KCSO's helicopter will get the climbers any minute. The two of them are at the Thumbtack, a rock finger in the middle of the basin below Chair Peak, waiting to be winched out.

Standing in the upper parking lot, I can see the grey shadows of the mountains close around, and the blackness of sky above them. It seems quieter than usual. I stand in the dark, scuffing my ski boot back and forth on a chunk of rotten black ice, holding my car keys, trying to decide what to do. I could leave now, pick up a precooked chicken, and save dinner.

But I can't help thinking that alpinists always make it out. They suck it up, tape ice tools to splint their ankles, spit blood, and crawl out. Not all types of backcountry users do this. But climbers do. If a climber calls and says he's dragged his friend a hundred meters down toward the Thumbtack where he suspects it'll be easier for a helicopter to get to him, it means his friend is really hurt.

The door of the command van is closed to keep the heat in. I know the deputies hate it when we open the door and let the heat out, but I knock on the door of the RV anyway. My conscience isn't going to let me leave.

"Hi," I say.

"Keep the door closed!" he calls out. I close the door, but I close it with me inside it.

"I'm with Seattle Mountain Rescue. I know the helicopter will probably pick these guys up before we could get there, but what are your thoughts about sending a small team of skiers in to provide a backup, just in case for some reason they can't make the pick, just as a bet-hedger? I can make that happen for you." I don't tell him that I'm concerned that if the helicopter can't winch and we don't start now, the climber will die because it will take us too long to get there.

Working with new deputies can be tough. Some of them aren't psyched to be stuck with a bunch of volunteers. Volunteers can be hit-or-miss. I don't know this deputy well enough to guess his thoughts, but I'm pretty sure we both know that volunteerism can sometimes entail a strong desire to do a job that will most likely be marginally useless, or at best, insignificantly helpful, and that volunteers can occasionally fall prey to undue self-importance. I worry that perhaps he thinks this is one of those times.

He sighs, looking at his watch, calculating how much longer he'll have to stay here while he waits for us to ski back to the trailhead once the climbers are winched out. But he gets overtime to sit here. "Fine. Go if you want."

I know how to be a good backup plan, the craftsman-style non-power-tool backup plan I've spent my life learning. I become more familiar with this backup plan every year. Being the backup plan means my crew skis or climbs or trail runs toward the climber and then stays with him, ready to carry him out until he is literally flying away, especially if he's critically injured, because I'm a climber and I want to hedge the bet so he doesn't die.

I've skinned halfway up to Source Lake, headed toward the Thumb-tack, when the helicopter circles for the last time, radios down to base that the swirling winds are going to prevent a pick, and flies off.

Drew has been skinning right behind me. "Yeah," he says, as an apology, laughing but not really. "I just don't feel good, like I guess I've just been drinking too much? But maybe I'm coming down with a cold or something. I've just been getting winded lately. Must be the proof I'm finally over the hill."

"You're not over this hill," I tell him. "Keep those legs movin'. "

We keep going, but I hear Drew groaning behind me. Drew's rappel anchor failed coming down from this same peak a few years ago, on a night like this. Drew dragged himself down to the Thumbtack with a broken femur, and Russell carried him out. That's why Drew joined SMR in the first place. The queasiness he's feeling now could

be a flashback. Or it could just be that even though Drew is a slender guy, he is in his fifties, and maybe he just can't keep up with me.
But I can't kick back the pace, because I think this climber is dying.
I see Drew's headlamp behind me, and then I see it faintly blinking
through the snow-caked trees, and then I can't see it at all.

Four months after this Chair Peak avalanche deal, Drew will say
he's tired again. We'll be jogging up Tiger Mountain to get a hiker
with a broken ankle. On that day, Drew thinks maybe he's coming
down with something. Feels breathless. Sweaty. Nauseated. A few
hours later I'll go to bed and then wake up from a dream about
poutine—just a long shot of gravy being poured over French fries and
cheese curds—and realize I'm an idiot, and Drew shouldn't have any
fitness issues, and really, his symptoms back at the avalanche on Chair
looked a lot like angina.

So I get back up and call Drew, because I know Drew stays up late,
and I finally realize it's an emergency.

"Yeah, hey!" said Drew, "Nah, I'm good. I'm still just, like, wasted
and I feel like I'm running uphill while I'm sitting on my sofa, like
sucking air, um . . . but I'm self-medicating with some red wine, and
that's totally helping, so it's all good."

I listen silently, sitting at my dining room table and stabbing a
ballpoint pen into the back of my hand over and over like penance
for being a fucking idiot. Drew is going to survive due to a rapid
intervention of modern medicine, but it's going to force me to think
about how much I'm focused elsewhere, blind to what helping people
I barely know can cost the people I do.

That's all later, though. Tonight, Drew's somewhere behind me,
and between us there's just ice and no discernible track. To orient
myself, I look up for the blacker outline of Chair Peak against the
blackness of the clouds, but I can't see it. All is darkness.

I look down, and it's still dark. My headlamp has a short. Again.
They never last very long—rain gets into them and corrodes stuff. I
flick it with my finger, and mercifully it turns back on so I can see the
snow again under my skis in the Source Lake basin. I keep skinning
like the devil is catching up with me.

It's super icy above Source Lake. Too icy to ski without crampons.
Windswept and hard, but finally I see the climbers ahead of me. And

they see one headlamp coming toward them. One blinking headlamp with what appears to be a short. I look at my watch, and it's ten minutes before ten.

Universally, in my experience, the people we rescue look up from their cold huddle of misery and say, "Can you call the helicopter back?" But if the helicopter pilot could have winched them out without feeling like he was going to crash, then he would have done it.

If I say, "I'm sorry," I'm worried they'll think I'm responsible for its absence. If I say everything will be okay without it, I'd be lying. Helicopters are great, sexy, throbbing machines of destiny. This climber thought he was going to be at Harborview Medical Center in half an hour, going to live. He was about to be fixed, or at least be pain free for a while.

Instead, he's stuck with me. I'm kind, but not particularly sexy, and I come with no assurances except to say that we will do the best we can.

Once the professionals show up, injured people start to deteriorate. They can compensate successfully for a long time on their own, and then I guess they just let go when they see rescue coming. So I think the fact that I don't look like a convincing rescue usually works in my favor. But this time, when I get close to the climber I can tell that, no matter what, keeping him alive all the way back to the trailhead might be beyond my skill level.

I look down into the valley and tell him that it'll be four hours, optimistically, back to the parking lot at Alpental if we can ski the lower part of the trail through the Commonwealth. It's too icy and steep to ski above Source Lake tonight with a toboggan, icy enough we're going to have to lower him one rope length at a time.

I tell him that he is four hours from help, and he has to hold on until then.

I give him my −20-degree sleeping bag, a sleeping pad, and my jacket. I have sweet hot tea in a thermos, and I hand it over to his partner.

These two guys are better climbers than I am. They're also both nurses, and they've already done any first aid I can do. They outline the damage, and I key the mike on my radio and relay it. I have some medical supplies, but it's too windy to even bother pulling out my stethoscope, though I want to.

"Base. Team 1," I call over the radio, "I need the next team out to bring up some more oxygen."

The climbers tell me they already looked for blood and didn't find any. It's way too cold for me to take off anyone's jacket to look at stuff they already told me is or isn't there, and I can't fix anyway. I tell the injured climber to tell me if anything gets worse. He says he will. I manage this minute of activity and then we're just waiting, us and the cold, tart, swirling winds, until more people show up.

I need the gear from our truck and a dozen strong folks, and we need to go right now. I keep scanning the low, white roll below us, looking for lights, trying to do anything but look for stuff that isn't there, so I look up at the sky.

"Well, check that out!" I say, "the Beehive nebula." I sound confident when I point to it. No way they're climbing-nurse-stargazers. I need to look like I'm good at something, and right now that something is small talk.

This injured climber, he is well-connected. He called 911 after the avalanche, but he called his friends first. When Drew finally crests the rise, he's followed by people I can't recognize, but it turns out that the lights belong to a small cadre of guides and professional climbers. They've brought Sherpa tea, which is a fair sight better than Wild Berry Zinger. We all switch over to drinking the Sherpa tea immediately.

I am happy, but also worried for a second. I dated a guide once. He had to be in charge of everything. He couldn't turn off the guiding. I was a better climber than he was, but we were never partners. We broke up and he found bliss with a woman who didn't lead.

Plus, guides learn a lot of small-party rescue techniques—like how to turn skis and poles into an emergency sled using nothing but athletic tape, a ski strap, and a Northwest Avalanche Center trucker's hat, and that's admirable—but this wasn't that sort of deal.

I was also worried about the guides because I feel like any decent climber knows the SAR stereotype: We're Bishop J. Dudley Love and his gun-toting Search and Rescue Squad from the Monkey Wrench Gang. We're aligned with park rangers and all sorts of law enforcement groups. We're fat white men in our sixties who wear neon vests, and make jokes about who has the biggest radio antenna. We're not climbers. The reason these guide friends were here in the first place was because they felt they could do a better job by their friend without ever having met me.

But I haven't been a park ranger for over ten years, and different types of volunteers are good at different things. I've done this so many times. So many times right here; I want to go with my plan. Now I see the twinkling lights of my crew below us. They were probably wearing NWAC trucker's hats too, but they also had ninety pounds of rescue-specific equipment with them, borne in on legs shaped by a similar love of the mountains. They'd be here in five minutes.

I'm not sure where to go with this one. I say I'm a climber. Actually, as the guides approach, I might even yell it, waving my arms in the air like a maniac, just to impress the point that I climb way more days than I rescue people. Then my headlamp shorts out again, and I realize that the jacket I'm wearing is four years old, and I brought the wrong kind of tea—totally not trendy—and my backpack isn't even a ski backpack, it's a hiking backpack because that was what was already packed when the initial text came out, and I just don't look good in trucker hats. Normally these things don't matter because my crew knows me, but I know that tonight I'm not going to be able to prove competency by first impression.

I switch tracks, pull out my radio with the shoulder mike. I've gotten it programmed to say, "Dude," when I turn it, but I don't say that. I wave it around in the air while talking loudly back and forth with the gun-toting deputy in base about how I'm going to be in charge.

But I don't have to worry; one of them comes up to me, takes off his trucker hat, scratches his head, and asks what they can do to help out. They are strong and sure, and I like them. They just want to help their friend. They hadn't been sure anyone from SAR could ski, or could actually hike this far for that matter, and so, yeah, they'd come to save their buddy from the avalanche, and from us; but now they're willing to give me a shot, and throw in. I'm grateful for this, and grateful too that Patrick, Larry, Garth, and the rest of my crew arrive right behind them with medical supplies, a litter, and ropes. They go to work, and I don't have to say anything but hello.

We all know it's a race. A race we are only going to win with the help of the climber's fortitude, and a team of craftsmen who have spent their lives working their way through the mountains in one way or another. It's not sexy, but I think it's beautiful. Maybe it's exhaustion that makes people not judge each other anymore. Nobody cares about brands, or gender, or status, or labels—just the deftness of hands working in the dark, chipping this ice, untying this knot. There is only the burn when you can't let go. The burn becomes the only reality, and it's universally understood. Being able to direct this level of purpose is humbling. I point out anchors, control speed and direction, talk to the folks making more anchors down below us. It doesn't take many words:

"Down."

"Twenty feet."

"Almost there."

"Perfect."

I can smell sweat in the cold as the litter passes me, four guys working as hard as they can to keep it on track toward the next anchor, more than a few degrees off the fall line.

I can't read music, but I imagine this is a little bit how a conductor feels. Picking the score, and then—I just move lights in the dark. Deft, sure-footed, focused lights. All of my best friends and new friends, working together on a dozen different projects simultaneously with one goal, and tonight we're going to win. I can't help but love to watch them. We are a symphony for one man. The kind of orchestra that knows closing night is coming, and they're playing their hearts out for the joy of doing the work together. I hope he can hear it.

Together we lower the climber 600 feet down the fall line, traverse to avoid a cliff, then lower another 1,200 feet using a mix of buried skis for anchors higher up, and trees once we hit tree line. Larry and Garth run ahead and build anchors so that the litter never stops moving. In the basin we chop out as much of the ski track as possible.

Then it's a mile and a half of side-hilling traverse to the parking lot, all of it compacted into bulletproof ice and steeply angled by the scraping of a thousand skis all taking the same line. We tie webbing for hand lines on the litter, but standing on the uphill side still means booting with tenuous footing in a bad line, and keeping the litter from sliding down and into the stream at the bottom. It's like holding a lead birthday balloon by a string, and hoping not to get carried away.

Finally, we slide into the parking lot. The climber goes with the medics. Weeks later, he gets out of Harborview and goes home. A year later, his wife gives birth to a daughter.

I look at my watch. It's 3:30 a.m. Russell leaves for work at five. I have to get home for Vivi. My car is so cold, much colder than the woods were. My hand on the stick shift is numb. Some of the 4x4 rescue guys are watching me, leaning against their light bars. They're in their sixties, their neon vests bristling with radios, and they're probably wondering how this is going to turn out. I push in the clutch with my left foot, turn the key, and take a deep breath.

The car lurches forward, shudders, and dies. I don't care. I just spent all night keeping a guy alive, and that was a lot harder.

Driving down the pass, listening to Dirty Vegas's "Days Go By" over and over again, I decide that I like being in the mountains because the mountains don't care. Sure, we do, but they don't care who you are. Injured people don't care either. This dying man, he didn't care that I was a volunteer, or a woman; he probably didn't notice. All he needed was someone to be with him, and all I had was the time to do it, and that was enough.

OTTER FALLS

ALL OF THESE STORIES START the same way. I'm always doing some mundane thing, making pasta, or brushing my teeth, or maybe something motherly, reading my kid a story or helping her with her homework. Suddenly, I get the call. I'm home, and then I'm running off to try to rescue someone, and then I'm limping home again. It's a formulaic microcosm. But, of course, my life is not just those times. I do lots of other things, joyful things, too, alpine climbing, backcountry skiing, and kayak-camping with Vivi. I hope these impressions of sun-drenched rock, sunsets with friends, boxed wine, and smores are written as indelibly in my memory.

What kind of person wants to read about rescues that failed? And what does it say about me that I wrote these stories down? To say this day, or that day, didn't matter would be disrespectful to whoever died. It mattered. But if I say I saw something bad, does that make me a pretentious fool with a small understanding of the world's tragedies? This story isn't about a war, or a plague. It doesn't take place anywhere iconic, and it didn't happen for a cause. The world is full of grieving, and I spent a few hours in one corner of it, and this was a thing I saw in between waking and breakfast. And this is another thing I saw in between eating dinner and brushing my teeth. That's all.

Steve and I crouched outside the door of the yellow-and-white Cessna. The two men and one woman inside it were dead, hanging upside-down from their seats, still strapped into their seat belts. We stabilized the plane before crawling in, tied webbing to the fuselage to keep it from moving farther down the slope while we were still partially in it. Crime scene tape was strung up between the trees, and two dozen SAR folks stood on one side or the other. The National Transportation Safety Board was satisfied that enough photos had been taken, and gave us the green light to take the bodies out. On the news, bodies are always covered by yellow sheets, but we don't have a supplier for those. There's just us and them, and nothing in between.

It's one thing to tell someone to take the bodies out of a crashed plane, and another thing to do it. On my climbing harness I carry a knife the size of my pinky finger, but I didn't have it with me.

Finally, I said, "I'm just going to unbuckle the seat belt." It turns out that this isn't a good thing from the NTSB's perspective; they prefer to have seat belts cut, because that way they can confirm that they were buckled, but I didn't know that at the time. It had been four years since the last plane crash I'd found, and there the seats, the seat belts, and the people were no longer separately defined.

"I'm ready," said Steve, and he lay down on the ceiling of the plane so that when I hit the release, the dead woman would be cushioned in his arms.

Steve is in his fifties. He's an engineer, and looks the part: conservative haircut, nerdy retro glasses, a mechanical pencil always in his breast pocket. He's the kindest person I've ever met, and I call him for fatherly advice every time I get into a sticky spot in any aspect of my life. He's really good at doing the right thing.

Steve has two sons. The youngest still lives at home. Steve and his boys were in the Boy Scouts together, and they joined ESAR—the Explorer Scout arm of King County SAR—together, too, before Steve finally joined SMR when his sons were grown. His older son got married and bought a house a block from Steve. They both own teardrop trailers, each with a little bed covered with a hand-made quilt, and a tiny hatchback kitchen setup. They go to tear-drop trailer conventions together, where Steve tells me that they sit around a campfire in aluminum retro camp chairs, and then go out for pancakes in the morning. The passengers in the plane were the same age as Steve's sons.

The weather at the plane crash site was on-again, off-again rain with intermittent fog. The fire department was going to try to hike up and fell some trees near the plane to make a space large enough that a helicopter could winch the bodies out. The plane had crashed at 4 a.m., and it was 10 a.m. now. We weren't sure that it would clear up again, and if we ended up carrying all three passengers out by hand, it was going to take the rest of the day. So, considering the uncertainly of all other options, we decided to start now.

We laid the people from the plane in a line, each in a military surplus body bag, the drab green ones with a white plastic liner like a zippered shower curtain. I picked the one closest to the trailhead and we started to carry him down, four at a time, taking turns when our arms got tired.

The police had closed the trail and we were alone except for a cell phone ringing. It rang over and over, and finally we recognized that it belonged to the young man we were carrying. It was crazy that it still worked after the crash. The phone rang for what seemed like an hour. It would ring, go to voicemail, and then ring again.

"I have to make it stop," said Steve, and so we paused. He unzipped the bag and patted through the kid's pockets until he found the phone and pulled it out. The caller ID said, "Dad." Steve looked at it for a while and then placed it, still ringing, back in the pocket.

Once we got the first body down, we grabbed sandwiches from base—one of the 4x4 guys had done a Safeway run—and hiked back up to get the second one. While we were hiking, the helicopter managed to find a break in the weather and fly out the two other bodies, so we turned around and headed back down again.

That was in February. Four days later, we got called for a snow-boarder who fell off a cliff at Alpental and died. En route we were diverted to Stevens Pass for an avalanche that killed three people, but by the time we'd driven from near Snoqualmie Pass to Stevens, the Stevens ski patrol, who handled the recovery in a more timely manner than we could, diverted us to a woman potentially having a heart attack in the backcountry near the resort at Stevens Pass. After we'd gotten her out, we stood in the parking lot with our hands in our pockets, and then went back into the resort and asked if they'd comp us night skiing passes because we had just driven for five hours in a state of high anxiety in a large circle around the county, and we needed to ski together. And they did, because they're awesome.

Winter turned to spring, and spring into summer. Someone completed a suicide off of Rattlesnake Ledge, and Caley, Russ, and I helped carry him out. A fluffy black-and-white dog got stranded for two days on top of the Haystack on Mount Si, and Steve lured her with lunchmeat. We lowered Steve from the top, and he picked her up off a tiny ledge and held her until they reached the bottom. She was quiet the whole time, but once she was down and free, she turned around and bit through the web of his hand. Steve said it hurt, but he didn't blame her. Then a woman fell from the top of a sport climbing route at Exit 38. We went out for a myriad of broken ankles and bum knees. A family of eight called because they believed they were being stalked by a bear on Tiger Mountain, and another woman said that her dog was stuck after climbing up the side of a cliff on Mount Si, but failed to mention that she had climbed up to try to get her dog, and now she was stuck, too.

Vivian had pneumonia in September. Russell and I had been sea kayaking on the West Coast of Vancouver Island. She'd gotten sick after the first few days, and became lethargic; we'd taken to carrying her in our arms, even though she was big enough to walk to the bathroom, and so we knew we had to come home early. As soon as we got back, Russell started projectile vomiting and sweating through the sheets with a Norwalk-type virus. I moved Vivian to my mom's house so they wouldn't cross-contaminate each other, and I started sleeping in Vivian's bedroom, which is the nicest one in our old house. Her room has yellow lathe and plaster walls, and before Vivian was born my mother painted the ceiling midnight blue, with purple clouds and the Milky Way circling around a filigreed chandelier bedecked with chains of tiny glass balls and multicolored silk flowers.

I was there, reading in her bedroom at five minutes before eight in the evening, when the text came in from Pete the deputy: two badly injured hikers up the Middle Fork Valley. It said to come ASAP, with two exclamation points after it. We always come ASAP. Linde is not a new deputy. There have never been exclamation points before.

"I need to take your truck," I said to Russ, cracking open his bedroom door. "My car can't handle the Middle Fork Road." I texted Jenn, my neighbor, who also has a white Honda Fit, that I'd pick her up in Russ's truck in two minutes.

Caley was ahead of me. Over the radio he said that some kids had tried to climb Otter Falls, which are mostly dry at this time of the year, and they'd fallen. He'd run into the brother coming out to find help somewhere on the road.

Another teenager had tried climbing up Otter Falls a few months earlier, while it was still running. He'd used his bare toes to feel his way up the rocks under the thin cascade of water. But it was slippery, and he'd fallen into the pool at the bottom. Bystanders told me and the other rescuers that they'd performed CPR and the kid had miraculously gasped and sat up. "Just like they do on *Baywatch*," a woman said. A helicopter flew him out, because on *Baywatch* you're fine once you're miraculously revived, but that doesn't always happen in real life.

I knew this waterfall, because a few years earlier I'd helped carry a 375-pound man with a broken ankle out from there, balanced in the litter by our arms and a flattened bicycle wheel. The falls had been backdrop then, but on the day of the teen's fall I'd looked at the falls as a beautiful thing, and I'd judged how far it was from its convex swell down the slab to the pool, the angle of the rock, the cracks and ridges for handholds. That had been a hot summer day and the pool was blue with cold, swift water full of bubbles. I'd spent a long time there looking up at the falls, waiting with the teen, a couple of medics from Bellevue, and the bystanders until the helicopter finally showed up.

So I knew that it was 26.4 miles from my house to where the pavement and cell phone service end on the Middle Fork Road. It was 12 miles of rutted decayed track from there to the Taylor River Road to the trailhead, and 3.3 miles from the trailhead to Otter Falls. I knew how long it would take me to get there.

Tonight Jenn, one other SMR guy, and I were the second team behind Caley, who had left the trailhead fifteen minutes before us since he lives closer, in North Bend. Over the radio, without telling us the story, he told us to run. He was running, we could hear it; his mike sounded like it was caught under his shoulder strap, keying with every step over and over, creating rapid bursts of static. Jenn and I have weathered some interesting climbing trips together, but she hadn't been in SMR that long, and this was on-the-job training.

"Jenn," I said, "these are just kids."

We kept running for a minute. "Jenn," I said again. "This could be really bad."

Jenn's a children's librarian. She loves kids. "Tell me what to do," she said.

I was outrunning the light from my headlamp, running flat out through the dark. I couldn't see the rocks or downed trees across the trail until they were already behind me. Either I could fly, or some unconscious part of my brain told my feet where to land. We were breathing and moving in the dark as one, drawn forward almost against our will but needing the group's momentum to overpower the raw living energy of this place we're going. Sometimes it's enough. Sometimes, together, we have that power. And sometimes we don't, and we sit together, and get beaten.

The kids had decided to climb up the waterfall. It was mostly dry, an early fall dryness, the end of the snowmelt leaving only ground bees and a few smears of green damp belying the purpose of the falls: to facilitate gravity, creating awesome beauty or awesome devastation with absolute impunity.

The King County Sheriff's Office has a helicopter, and most of the time, when it looks like a helicopter would be helpful, it comes. But SAR also shares flight time with the county's SWAT team, so the helicopter is sometimes busy chasing down robbers with heat sensors. Maybe it was doing that, or maybe tonight it was out for maintenance, but it wasn't available. Once or twice a year, we have to find another helicopter, so Pete had called Snohomish County for reciprocity. We could hear it in the distance, coming, about the same time we saw the fire.

The place had changed since I'd seen it last. The helicopter was circling, blowing the trees in wild gyrations, and someone had lit a bonfire that flared enough to illuminate the pool, which was greenish-black now, and smaller, surrounded by logs and sticks and jumble that had come down the falls all season. A lot of people had been here; there were empty plastic water bottles, candy wrappers, and broken CDs, and a teenage boy lying at the water's edge.

"They fell from the top," said another teenager, whom I found out later was this boy's brother. I knew, since I'd seen it before, that the top of the sloping granite bed surface, where the waterfall would be if it were running, was about 300 feet above us.

Caley was trying to help the helicopter find a clearing big enough to winch down a paramedic. He yelled to me, trying to be heard over the rotor wash, that there was this injured boy, and another one on the far side of the pool.

I'm an EMT, which means I can splint legs. I can give peanut butter and jelly sandwiches to people with low blood sugar. Once I delivered a baby on the side of a road—I really did nothing, except try to be a calming influence, and then I handed the woman her baby. Even my partner knew there was nothing to be done.

"Pull over, come back here, and help me!" I'd said, popping my head through the tiny window into the front of the ambulance.

"Okay, I'll drive faster!" he replied.

This situation at the falls was just another one where I did not have the skills to alter the inevitable.

Later, Jenn said she was told there were four kids hiking together. Three climbed to the top of the waterfall. They got stuck, each in his own place on the undulating, damp rock. One fell, tumbled down the face and landed in the rocks at the base of the pool. The boy that hadn't climbed rushed around the pool and jumped into the water to hold the other's head up. He said his friend had been talking in the beginning, but then he stopped. After some time, a second boy couldn't hang on any longer and fell. Then the boy who hadn't climbed was holding onto both of them, not strong enough to pull them out of the water.

Somehow, the third boy climbed back down. Some hikers met him running out, and heard his story. One of them had a Forest Service radio and called out for help, which was how Linde found out, and then the hikers went back to help. They managed to drag one boy out of the water, made a bonfire, and sat with both kids while they were dying, because there was nothing else they could do, either. The third boy kept running, and he ran into Caley just as Caley arrived at the trailhead.

The helicopter finally found a spot, and winched down a paramedic in a black jumpsuit, and another guy in an orange jumpsuit.

This paramedic was a man of few words. "Okay, he's dead," he said to me, the kid's brother standing at my shoulder. Then he turned away.

I got pissed about it later, and called the paramedic after a week because I thought he could have said something to the dead kid's brother. A word, an explanation. Once I heard an interview on NPR about a paramedic who'd been at the scene of a crime where a woman had just been bludgeoned to death with a baseball bat by her daughter's boyfriend in the middle of the night. He said he'd just kept yawning, because it was late and this wasn't anything he hadn't seen before; but afterward, he worried that he was losing some part of his ability to feel empathy. To feel connected. That scared him. He quit.

But this paramedic explained to me over the phone that he was a professional paramedic as his day job, he was a real first responder, and he dealt with death every day, and I wouldn't understand. He felt that I was having a problem with what I saw because I was unused to death. He told me death bothers people who aren't used to it, that I was an amateur.

Both boys were dead. The paramedic and the orange jumpsuit thanked us for helping them out, winched back into their helicopter, and flew off.

Aaron and Steve showed up with more than a dozen ESAR people. Caley had to go. He had a meeting at work in the morning that he could not miss. Because professional life doesn't understand this life—doesn't know why it's important for us to be here. He told base I'd take over as field leader, and left. I didn't need to be an EMT anymore, so I pulled out a notebook and my radio, said goodbye to Caley, and then I was Team 1 and responsible for all of this.

"Radio relay. Team 1." Base couldn't hear me, the Middle Fork has terrible comms, but one of the 4x4 guys with a huge whip antenna on his truck was parked at the end of the road, and could pass on my message.

"I need another litter and wheel, two body bags, all the personal flotation devices in base, a camera, and a bicycle pump."

The litter wheel I've got is flat, and the pump is missing. I put Steve in charge of staging the ESAR people away from the pool in the woods, and carrying the boys out when we were ready.

"Okay," Steve finally said, "let me know when you're ready for us."

I pointed to the brother and the hikers, and asked Jenn to interview them about what had happened, and write everything down.

Then there was a hang-up with the medical examiner. Base wanted us to wait to do the recovery, saying the ME might need us to do some specific documentation beyond photographing everything, or the ME might want to come out himself, but he had a few other cases he needed to deal with first.

It was already after midnight. "We can't wait much longer," I said. More folks were going to have to start leaving for work, and we'd need everybody to carry the boys out. Base said they'd be able to get more information about the time frame, in about two hours.

My crew that night was two med students, a children's librarian, and an engineer, as well as the dead boy's brother and three shirtless hikers—shirtless because they'd pulled off their T-shirts for bandages, and used one to make a tourniquet with a stick as a windlass. We sat down on the ground in a huddle, and watched the fire. The brother, who looked like he was maybe fifteen, was quiet. We were quiet, but I should have said something, explained something, or else I'm a hypocrite to wish the medic had. But as an amateur I couldn't find the language. I mean, I could talk about the process of death, but it wasn't about the physical anymore. Now I wanted some words to say, or a tradition of some sort to mark the gravitas of death, some action that humans do for each other in this moment. To do the thing that their parents would want. But I didn't know what that thing would be, and I didn't want to do the wrong thing. So we just sat together, with our backs hunched against the night, until base finally said we could start. I should have had Steve stay with us instead of organizing for the evac; maybe he would have known what to say.

The body bags never showed up, but the ESAR folks had brought some blue tarps, and we wrapped the body on the near side of the pool. I asked the brother to go out with Steve, because being with Steve is the most stable place on nights like this. Then the rest of us went to get the other boy back from the rocks at the far side of the pool.

The pool's edge felt like slimy, low fifth-class climbing in the dark, at the limit of trail running shoes. Slipping meant falling into the pool, which was stagnant and instantly deep enough to be opaque. The brother had said it was deeper than his head. I was not going to touch the water.

But there was no way we could carry the boy across the rock. Aaron looked for a place to put an anchor above our heads so we could rig a rope system. But he found nothing. There was no other way. Aaron groaned and pushed his body back against the rock, as far from the water as possible. I don't hug people very often, but Aaron and I held each other for a minute because some things need the courage of more than one person. Or maybe because we're amateurs. Jenn just stared at her hands, wearing fingerless leather rope gloves with purple nitrile gloves underneath. Her fingers looked purple.

"They look inhuman," she said to me.

"They're not," I said back.

Finally, we asked the ESAR people if any of them had air mattresses; they usually carry at least some camping gear. I could see blood in the water. Blood like creamer descending into coffee and then diffusing. I couldn't tell if it was fire or blood that made the whole green pool look red. The multitudinous seas incarnadine.

As my friends worked I kept saying, "You can do this. You're okay. You're doing good work." But I didn't know if I was really talking to them, or to myself.

After a while, Aaron said in a strangled voice, "I think he's gotten tangled on branches in the water, but I don't want to pull any harder. I don't want to hurt him."

We got the boy to the other side.

We extinguished the fire and it was cold, but a relief.

I didn't try to hike out with either litter team. Everyone was self-sufficient at this point, and they could call me on the radio if they needed anything. I walked out by myself, between them.

We got back to the trailhead at ten minutes past three in the morning. Everyone melted away, headed to work. I didn't see them again, just headed for the command van and started my part of the paper-work. I wrote a two-page report that said nothing.

I drove out of the parking lot at 4:30, feeling jealous of the people who had to go to work, because for them there was some purpose in this next day, some goal they could focus on achieving. Maybe it's as simple as, if you have to keep moving, even when you're exhausted, at least you don't have to stop. Or maybe it's like when Vivi was a baby, she was colicky. She'd scream all day and all night, and all I wanted was to stop listening to the screaming, and the idea of going to work actually seemed like it would be a relief.

It was too early to go to my mom's to visit Vivian, so I went home and quietly closed the front door behind me. When the morning sun comes through the window into my daughter's yellow room, it hits the wall and glows crinkly and gold under the Milky Way. Her pillow smells like her drool and banana hair conditioner. I climbed into her bed and spooned her three-foot tall stuffed penguin. I couldn't sleep, but I spent a long time staring at the wall, just thinking how beautiful the sunlight was.

I also looked up the definition of amateur. It means unskilled per-son. It also means somebody who loves something.

SNOQUALMIE FALLS

TODAY I'M AT THE GROCERY store. I forgot my phone on the kitchen table, but I have my volunteer fire fighter pager, and my fire department volunteer chaplain pager—I know, it's a bit of an odd choice, and I'm not religious. I'm a fire chaplain now, because fire chaplains don't get messed with by fire fighters, which is really helpful for surviving volunteering long enough to get a job. But I also wanted to be a chaplain because I thought I might be more useful doing that than cleaning the fire station and being the fourth person in the aid car responding to the occasional sprained ankle. As a fire chaplain, I spend a lot of time sitting with families, going through old photo albums, waiting for the medical examiner or a car from the funeral home to show up. Pretty similar to what I do with SMR, mostly just listening and being present.

I don't know how many dead people I've found doing SAR. Not that many, compared with professionals who deal with death. Perhaps I've found or carried out eighty people over the years. With notes. Without notes. Dead by guns. Hangings. Pills. Suicides. Accidental death. Hypothermia. Falls. It feels a bit like being a midwife, but for death.

It's a weekday, but Russell has the day off. He's been up in our attic, trying to rewire the ceiling above the dining room. Insulation gets everywhere, with him climbing in and out. The lath and plaster is so fragile, he touched it with his foot at one point and a foot-wide chunk of plaster cracked off and landed next to our bedroom door.

When I get home the plaster is still there, but he is gone. I bring in the groceries and start putting them away when the phone beeps. "SMR and ESAR OLs call Ed. Recovery bottom of Snoqualmie Falls." Time stamped twelve minutes ago.

It's odd, now that I think about it, that we get called to Snoqualmie Falls, since it's not in the mountains. It's a tourist attraction between Carnation and North Bend, nine miles from my house: a 268-foot waterfall visited by 1.5 million people a year. On one side is a four-star luxury hotel and spa; on the other, a hydroelectric power plant. The City of Snoqualmie has a paid fire department with the ropes and skills to retrieve the bodies of people who jump, but they have a policy that they will only go over the falls to rescue someone who's still alive; they won't risk the lives of their guys if there's no hope left.

I don't think anyone has ever survived going over these falls. I can't imagine it'd be possible. That's the whole point of jumping.

I call Russell, and he's already halfway there, making sure that SMR-1 shows up because it has 600-foot ropes. Our regular 300-foot ropes won't be long enough.

I call my mother-in-law and arrange for her to pick up Vivian after preschool.

The strangest thing to me is that nobody jumps over the waterfall. Once, on a night when the river was very low, and a tree had crushed part of the hurricane fence on the far side, I climbed over the fence and waded out. There's a jut of rock at the edge of the falls in the very middle that rises above the waterline, and I stood on this rock and looked over the edge. It was breathtaking. But everybody jumps over the rail and off the gorge's edge from a little park next to the falls instead. Sure, it's a big cliff, and a sheerer drop than most, but you land on a grassy slope next to the waterfall and then roll downhill for a while. There used to be a covered lookout at one end of the park, and people would jump from there, but a few years ago they remodeled the park and took out the lookout. So now people jump from different random places along the trail.

There used to be a little gazebo that we could use for a high-directional, to help make the edge transition safer when we were lowering people down and bringing them back up, but the gazebo is gone now, too. For a while we could still use some pine trees growing out near the edge, but then one day they were all cut down, I guess because they didn't go with the landscaping. And now, going off the edge is scary. It crumbles under your feet, spilling huge rocks off into the gorge.

The parking lot at Snoqualmie Falls is crowded with tourists even though it's a Wednesday. Every day it doesn't rain, it's packed, and when it does rain, even more people come to see how large the falls can get. When we have flooding, this place is always on the local news.

It was a young woman who jumped. We do the math quickly, independently in our heads, and check it on my smartphone. She weighs a few pounds too much to lower two people down to get her in a litter and help keep her body off the rock on the way back up. Our two lightest people plus the woman would exceed the safety margin on the breaking strength of our equipment. So I tie into the ends of two long-tailed bowlines, and tuck a number of biohazard bags and a digital camera in a Ziploc bag that the medical examiner handed me under the litter straps, and then I lean back over the edge by myself.

The canyon walls are disintegrating. The moment I go over the edge my feet start knocking off shale chunks the size of microwaves. This is a new spot we haven't cleaned yet. I have them hold me dangling there, so Russ can hand me a shovel, and then I start prying at the edge.

A lot of rock falls into the canyon. Eventually, I pry enough that the remaining rocks have a fairly firm connection to the dirt; then I have them lower me the rest of the way, dodging under the litter as rocks rain down around me, whacking the litter or flying by with a whirr. If one of the big ones hit me, I'd be dead. But they miss. Some of the smaller ones do hit me, but it won't hurt until tomorrow.

Sometimes I think about what happens when a fire fighter dies in a line-of-duty death, a LODD; I've learned about it in chaplain training. The massive crush of brotherhood, support, and honor for their fallen hero, and the ultimate sacrifice for the work they do. The governor comes, and thousands offer respect from all over the country.

But I'm just here sometimes, in this place, in that place. Some places are dangerous, but it's not like my job is dangerous because, technically, I don't have a job. A friend of mine sells insurance, and I was looking into getting life insurance, and he laughed and said it wasn't worth it because I'm not, technically, worth anything.

As I continue to lower down, the dirt goes from dry to wet to mucus-covered rocks. Normally, I walk my feet down while being lowered, but here at a certain point I have to leave my feet out in front of me, and they slide down through green slime. I keep going, and it's just rock. The water blowing over from the waterfall is like an aqua massage at the mall. It's hard to see, and hard to breathe. Sometimes, since they generate power at the sub station, they can turn the falls down so there is less spray pounding down, but it's been raining too hard, the river is too high, and it isn't safe to turn down the volume today.

For me it's always startling to have a whole group of people suddenly working to support me, when most of my days I'm just working to support Russ and Vivi in the most mundane ways of sandwich-packing and vacuuming. But doing this helps me feel like, even if I'm not that valuable in real life, right now I have a skill that I can use to help someone; it's the same skill set it takes to be a mom: Ubuntu, sharing the universal bond that connects humanity so that no one feels alone. Creating a connection. For now, I still have time to be here and do this. And for this moment, it feels like it's enough. This is something that I know how to do as well as anyone does. This isn't rescuing anyone. I'm here volunteering to help this woman with the decision she's made. Not try to fix anything, just be here.

No raingear is enough. I'm instantly soaked to the skin, and at the bottom I can barely see with so much water blowing in my face. She's lying on her side behind me, facing me, but although her lower jaw is there, and her lips, there's only a hole where the rest of her face should be, and some blond wavy hair matted down with a piece of white skull next to it. I pull out the camera. I can't see through the viewfinder because of the bag and the spray, and I don't want to see, either, so I look without looking. I take pictures of her head, her body—her legs folded up, her hands together, palms up. Her shoes a few feet away.

Who do you have to be in order to be the right person to do this? Who would I want to do this for me? I don't know her—her traditions, her values, her family. Should I be doing something that I'm not? This is one of the most intimate and vulnerable moments of this woman's life. It should be her mother doing this, and in this way I feel that it's not the job of a professional, not the job for someone acting with detachment and black humor and the support of a thousand buddies, and a thousand more bodies to collect down the line. This is a job for a human, not a hero, a human who has nothing else to do today but this. And I think it's a good thing that I can be here, that there are so many people like me who are here today.

Bodies are often heavy, untenable shapes, but she isn't. I hold her narrow white wrists and lift her torso into the litter, then lift her ankles to angle the rest of her body in. I don't have a body bag, it's too hard to try to get her into one by myself, so we'll do that at the top behind a tarp. I have a red biohazard bag, and I invert it and start picking up teeth, parts of the bones of her face, white and clean, even after only a few hours of the pounding water. I can't get all of them because the rocks are so slippery and steep down to the broiling water at the falls's base, and I can't see because of all the water in my eyes.

I tell her that the falls are an ancient burial ground for the Snoqualmie Tribe, who believe that the mist rising from the base serves to connect heaven and earth.

The litter is full of water; she is nearly floating in it as the water pounds down. When they raise us back up, water pours down on me over the rail and through the crack where the front and back half of the litter come together. Gallons of water and I'm silent, holding onto her, rising back up with the mist.

INFINITE BLISS

ONE NIGHT I FOUND A plane crash. The pilot and nine skydivers had known what it was to fly, their fingers holding the wind, directing them in fluid sweeping arcs. Now, along with the plane itself, they'd become one solid thing struck deeply into the earth. I got too close, wearing a Seattle Mountain Rescue jacket wrapped around me like an imaginary barrier. At the edges of the plane, the dirt was so soft my trail-runners sank into it—I could feel the turned earth tossed with jet fuel, humanity, and biotite mica sparkling in the dark, encircling the bare skin of my ankles. That was the night of the day I woke up and knew I was pregnant with my daughter.

I still wrestle gear into my subcompact car every few days to try to help someone, and I'm still spending much of my life wearing an apron with tiny red cherries printed on it. Still filling out job applications. Vivian's proud because she can climb in a skort. I think skorts and harnesses are a difficult wardrobe combination for anyone, but perhaps all it takes is confidence.

Vivian's enrolled in the Little Rockers program at the local climbing gym. She and her classmates take turns making their way up to touch the coveted tyrannosaurus hold. Other times, the instructors hang a rope from the ceiling like a giant swing, and the kids spend the hour careening back and forth. I take pictures. I get a photo of her swinging upside down, my spread-eagled fledgling in a state of bliss. I collect these images because moms have to document everything. But the photos don't convey how proud I am, or how scared that she'll become a climber.

After her first week of lessons, one of the instructors went climbing in the Alpine Lakes Wilderness, my home, on his day off. Coming down, he rappelled off the end of his rope and fell to his death.

I'd met this man, Ross, a number of times at the gym while he was putting up routes. He wore a muscle shirt and headphones. I always assumed he was listening to dance tunes. But I'm shy, so we never spoke.

I don't keep track of how many times I've gone to retrieve the body of someone I knew. Dozens, perhaps. Sometimes I think it's worse, knowing beforehand. I can't plan for the unknown, and ignorance makes it easier in the beginning.

We weren't sure where Ross had landed. Somewhere on Infinite Bliss, a route that winds its way up Mount Garfield. His climbing partner said a ledge on Pitch 10, or maybe Pitch 13, but for sure it was below Pitch 23. His partner had spent the night there, next to his body, and then she'd come down alone, making too many rappels to count, hiking out through the silent, damp woods, climbing over rotten deadfall, following a long mud track to the highway.

We hit road construction on the way, but the crews put culverts back in the roadbed to let us through. By the time we got to the trailhead, it was cool. The last of the year's mosquitoes floated around in the clammy air. The hike to the base involved climbing ladders of old-growth cedar roots, and crawling over and under deadfall along the indistinct climber's path. There had been bad rockfall on the route a few days before, damaging some of the bolts. A photo we found online showed mangled anchors. Finally, five of us stood in a line at the base, looking up. There is no easier route up the backside of Mount Garfield, and no reasonable way to descend from the top. We got a helicopter to fly over, but they couldn't see anything and the rock is too steep to hoist a body out even if they had.

The route is 2,600 feet of almost seamless granite. It's a sport climb, with permanent anchors and bolts drilled along the route. The steepest pitch is 10c, far below the ability of experts with natural talent, athletes sponsored by climbing shoe manufacturers, and AMGA-certified rock guides, but it isn't off-the-couch terrain for most folks, either. And it has some long runouts, which would be longer if bolts were missing, and there was no small measure of rain starting, and we're only as good as we are. Half the time, I go out to train when Vivian goes to bed, and I end up sitting alone on a log at midnight with wet running shoes, trying to find the energy just to get home, let alone work on cardio. Lately I've been making it to the climbing gym more than the crag, and climbing gets harder in the rain. We've got a bolt kit, but we have principles too, and the existence of this bolted climb in the Alpine Lakes Wilderness is already controversial enough. This climber we were going to get—I knew he wouldn't have wanted us to drill superfluously, out of fear.

So we decided we'd come back with more light. We weren't afraid, except for the unknown number of broken bolts and the possibility that more chunks of rock might calve off and come at us in the dark. And except for actually finding him. We've found people lots of times, but those experiences haven't made us any less wary.

"He died," I tell Vivian when I get home that night.

"When my fish dies, you said we could get a cat. I want a cat with orange spots," she says.

She's sitting on my lap with her eyes an inch from mine, and she's breathing on my nose. She has never even had a pet fish die.

"You'd be really sad if I died," I tell her. "His family is really sad, like that."

She's quiet for a minute. "If Daddy died, we could have a cat and a fish at the same time."

I hold her in my arms with her body against mine and my nose crushed into her ear, because this is how communicating with her happens. With intimacy and fear and effort. After a few minutes I tell her, "Grandma is going to pick you up from preschool tomorrow."

The next day, Vivian is at preschool—two hours of singing songs about the days of the week and identifying the weather. Larry, SMR's Chairman, called and offered to stay in base, run interference for me, and keep folks on track in a big-picture sense.

"Ed said he doesn't care what happens as long as you document the scene and run the recovery," says Larry. "He was all, 'I need someone up there I can trust.'"

"I hate it when Ed says that," I tell Larry. It just makes a bunch of other totally competent people upset. "Anyway, I'm pretty sure Ed doesn't trust anyone. At least, consistently."

"Don't worry about it," says Larry, "just figure out how to get the body back to the trail. Pick your team and put your plan together. Show up at six a.m. tomorrow. Cool?"

The rain's pounding up the mud in my garden. I sit at my kitchen table, surrounded by single-pane windows and old wood. I print out the topo and start thinking about the plan. A few hours later, I look down at the names of my dead friends that I've written in a line at the edge of the topo. Who wants their child to be a climber? Really?

Vivian did her first rescue with her daddy on Mount Pilchuck. They were ambling along, stopping a lot to look at bugs. She got one potato chip at each switchback. The day had been going well. Coming down from the lookout, she ran into a woman with a broken ankle. Vivian helped splint the ankle and keep the woman company for six hours until some of our friends arrived to carry her out. A few days later, the woman sent her a thank-you card. Vivian said she couldn't wait until she grew up so she could join Seattle Mountain Rescue, too.

In the morning, headed back to Infinite Bliss, I finally have to turn on my windshield wipers. But I wait as long as I can first, peering through the windshield while the road distorts into wavy streaks, because I know if I turn them on, I'll have to acknowledge that it is still raining.

Taylor, geologist-turned-MBA-student, Darby of the police tattoo, and I meet at the start of the closed road. Garth took the day off from serial birthday parties at Kidzbounce, and will spot for us. Larry continues to hold down the KCSO's Command RV with Ed the SAR Deputy.

I'm a little nervous because the three of us have never climbed together before. Because I woke up with a nasty head cold, and because Taylor says that he's dislocated his shoulder again this week, and he can't lift his arm any higher than his head. But he's confident that it's getting loose enough that if it pops out, I can help him pop it back in again. We also have to carry a bunch of rescue-specific gear including a SKED—an orange plastic stretcher—and we'll have to troubleshoot how to manage it all as we go. The SKED is heavy. We roll it up, but it's still so big that only the bottom half will fit in a backpack; the top half wobbles around and it makes it harder to balance on a damp slab route. But the guys are really good climbers, nowhere near the limit of their abilities, and it's good working together. Smooth. We average fifteen minutes a pitch.

I see Ross's shoe before I see him, lying under a weather-beaten tree at the edge of one of the few ledges. Ed gave me a camera, and I document everything for the medical examiner. But the photos don't convey what happened. To do this thing is to know the smell of blood running down granite as well as you know the smell of piss. Only a climber can look at a climber's fingers, survey the rock, and trace the fall. I touch his belay device first, kneeling under the tree with my feet above another thousand feet of space—just as easy to fall through. I look for the same things every time. I touch the gates on the 'biners, look for knots, cuts, gouges, fraying, backups, double-backing, shoes, gloves, everything. The absence of things. Once when I was young, someone handed me my friend's rack covered in feathers from a down jacket, glued on with dried blood. That doesn't have anything to do with this day except that that's the one that always stays with me.

I lift Ross in my arms with his body against mine because only a climber can get a climber back, and this is how that happens, the way everything happens in the mountains: with intimacy and fear and effort. It's not an act that you forget.

During most recoveries, I walk by the tight knot of family that invariably stands corralled next to the county sheriff's command van in a designated parking lot. I don't think—I've never felt—that we should meet, because what I do is public service. I should be invisible; I'm either a horrifying or an inconsequential person to them. But now they want to meet me, so they can thank me for bringing their baby home. But I brought their baby home dead. I stand next to Larry, or he stands next to me, all of us together in an awkward line. Ross's mother hugs me, and I don't know what to do with my face.

Ten minutes later, I'm kneeling behind a blue tarp held up by half a dozen people with their faces turned away, giving my report to the M.E. since he couldn't get the scene himself. I explain the basics of rock climbing, what the gear on his harness is for, how a climber stays attached to his rope, the position of his body, how it got there, and its condition. I hand over the pictures I took, and detail the parts that are significant. It's a courtesy, I suppose, but I've worked with enough M.E.s to know what they want. My hands are wet and half-frozen in blue nitrile gloves. The deputies want me to talk shop, and it's important to do this, but I'm looking for sanctity as much as reason. My mouth says, "flail chest," but my hand touching his chest says, *I am a mother like your mother, my daughter is a climber like you are a climber, and I will do my best by you.*

Doing this over and over means I have a good cognitive grasp of the physical and societal steps around death, but it doesn't mean I actually know what to do for the family, or for myself in the future. Maybe I know how I would feel if it were my child—but I don't think I do. I'm almost totally certain that you can't know the blinding pain of losing a child until you are blinded by it, and right now I'm just watching. Just being there.

Vivian took Ross's death better than I did. Whatever I'd managed to convey to her, she didn't pause. Days later, she broke her tiny arm bouldering. Jumping down, she extended spread-eagle, whacked her elbow and broke her humerus in two places. I watched her do it. She barely cried; it took serious investigation to find out she was really injured. She's still my baby, but she has the grit. It terrifies me. She got a hot pink cast up to her armpit, and she immediately figured out how to wedge it on the jungle gym at school and dead-hang off it.

I sat down at the kitchen table with a notebook and stared into space, thinking about a rack covered in drying, bloody feathers. Sticky. Then I got up again, put on the apron with the tiny cherries, and made a pie. Then I sat down. Then I got up and painted my fingernails black, called the climbing gym, and suspended Vivian's Little Rockers class until the cast came off.

LA BOHN GAP

IT'S OVERCAST, HUMID, BUT STILL cool in the slightly clammy way that means it will get hot as soon as the sun rises. Early Monday in August, and I would have slept later, sweating my way into this day in a string of listless days eventually spent listening to NPR and lying on the cool wood floor, drawing pictures of trees and flowers and cats that are indistinguishable from each other. But something woke Vivi early, and so we walked barefoot into the garden to pick blueberries for pancakes. And I held out the bowl and Vivi picked with great seriousness, one blue one, one pale greenish-white one, one leaf at a time placed in the bowl while I stood there waiting and looking up at the blank white sky.

I get the text at 6:51 for a missing trail runner out of Skykomish, and two minutes later another for three overdue campers in the Necklace Valley, a series of alpine lakes north of the Middle Fork and just south of Skykomish. This part of the Alpine Lakes Wilderness is not very far from my house as the crow flies, but I have to drive north and then east on Highway 2 for an hour to get there.

Yesterday I volunteered for the Fire Department, where being good is all about swiftly following orders, beginning the action before the words are completely out. Jogging to show purpose, even when I have nowhere to go. I get it. It's important not to waste the captain's time, or dawdle getting children overcome with smoke inhalation out of a burning building, although I can't really speak to that since I've never done it. But one thing I do know from long experience is that if you push a vacuum cleaner over a certain speed, it becomes ineffective.

I think the fire department wouldn't like Vivi, if they ever met her. I'll ask her to put her shoes on because we need to go to the store, and twenty minutes later I'll find her in her room surrounded by a sandstorm of little glass beads. When I ask her what she's doing, she says she needs to make a new necklace to match her shoelaces before she can put the shoes on. She gets crazy if I try to rush her, screams at me. So I help her pick out all the pink beads and string them together. I think maybe it's an important developmental thing, maybe some kind of basic math skill, or maybe just bonding, a way for her to be sure I'm paying attention. It takes so long sometimes that we don't make it to the store at all.

Russell gets angry at me when Vivian leaves her things out. He tells me that at real jobs, like the one I need to get, everyone pulls their weight, lives with concrete direction and purpose, and keeps their shit put away. I need to work on it, and so does Vivi because I'm not gearing her to be successful.

Maybe I could change her, but I just don't want to. It feels like I'd be destroying my own creation—her self-directed play, her creativity, moving from one discovery to another. Her interest in dirt, even though when you touch dirt, it tends to get everywhere. The space and time to just be together. I don't know what this unproductive time, what just being there for another human being when they're young, is worth.

But yeah, ostensibly I know it's worth nothing, and the whole world is about running. People think you must be a better person if you're busy. And I'm starting paramedic school the same day that Vivian starts kindergarten, so no matter how I feel about it, our days are numbered.

I need to pack for what could be a multiday search—the Necklace Valley is a big area—and feed Vivi some sort of breakfast, and find someone to watch her, and take her there, and then drive a little over an hour to meet at the Skykomish Ranger Station, and I need to be there right now.

I look down, and Vivi is digging in the dirt at the base of a blueberry bush, enthralled with the loaminess between her palms, and the smell of the plant. I know her stubborn desire for time to get to know this under-bushy place before moving on.

We have this secret life, where we just walk in the woods and then stop and listen with our eyes closed. I know this is bad. Everybody knows it won't be good cardio, and the mileage only counts under the purview of a GPS-enabled watch, recording the stopped time to make me aware of it so that I can minimize it next time. And never mind all of this; someone could die because I wasn't fast enough. It's like the hypothetical kids with smoke inhalation; sometimes speed really does matter. There's no time for Vivi to sniff blueberry bush roots.

I grab her sticky, stained fingers and lift her up in the air so that we're eye to eye, and I tell her, "Guess what? You get to eat your blueberries at GiGi's!"

She eyes me with suspicion. "Is there a mission? Make sure if I go to GiGi's that she takes me swimming."

I carry her back into the house, and that saves a few minutes. She is as fast at packing as I am. She packs her swimming suit and seven stuffed animals into four canvas shopping totes while I throw my backpack in the car. I carry her to her car seat and then run back in again to find her flip flops, a T-shirt and shorts so she's not stuck with her only clothes being a nightgown and a mint one-piece swimming suit with tiny white polka dots.

I find bits of information from the texts as I'm driving. It was a trail runner in his thirties. He'd parked his car at Alpental, planning to run north to Snow Lake, down the Rock Creek Trail, East on the Middle Fork Trail, over La Bohn Gap, and down the Necklace Valley Trail. Thirty miles and 7,800 feet of gain. He was doing a car swap with another trail runner, and that guy had successfully made the trip north to south without seeing him. That was yesterday, but still no sign of this trail runner. The car he should have picked up was still parked at the end of the dirt road, coated in dust streaked by evaporated rain.

Also, three guys in their twenties were overdue from a backpacking trip in the same area. The group planned to hike in to Trout Lake and then Big Heart Lake, followed by traversing the ridge to Tank Lakes, and then continuing down the Necklace Valley trail.

They're lost in a huge area. If those guys took the wrong trail, they could end up anywhere from Skykomish at the northerly end, to the south end at Snoqualmie Pass, or the Middle Fork Road out of North Bend to the west, or maybe Salmon la Sac out of Roslyn, all the way in the eastern half of the state. Folks are going to have to search all of these areas, but my mom lives roughly on my way to Skykomish, so I'll drop off Vivi and search from there first.

I'm going to meet up with Taylor at the Ranger Station in Skykomish. Taylor, still finishing up his MBA, has blown off class to come today. He was originally a friend of Aaron's—they met in the University of Washington's Climbing Club—that's how he found out about SMR. He's a little quiet, but laughs easily, and has a lithe athleticism equally well suited to climbing, running, or any other outdoor pursuit he chooses. I've always been struck by how kind and encouraging he is. I met his girlfriend once at a party. Taylor said they'd been together since grade school, and they thought from time to time about getting married, but he couldn't love her any more than he already did, or get any more committed, and his parents were hippies from Montana, so what was the point?

Big searches can be kind of fun to plan. When I first started searching for people, I would think about questions like, Where would I probably end up if I had an objective in mind but didn't make it there and back? What turns I would miss? Where would the highest likelihood for an accident be? After a while, I realized that other people almost never do what I would do myself. I quit guessing.

Working with statistics is easier. If the last ten people to get lost on Mailbox Peak all ended up in the same drainage, then it's easy to say that next time we should send a team down that drainage. But the most interesting part, always, is getting to interview someone's friends. Lots of times, friends who really know the person can look at the map, point, and say, "Right here." We look there.

I don't organize things in base so much anymore. Base jobs always involve sitting in a parking lot, thinking about what's going on, while the rest of my friends are out there dealing with the situation. I find it traumatic, like ancient Greek theater, where all the action happens off stage. Whatever I picture is probably worse than what's actually happening, but I don't really know.

Being in base makes me want to grasp at something physical, remove myself from the spiraling twilight zone of my own imagination. What works is the pain of stepping on a sharp rock while crossing talus. Or the cold of the bushes, their dew running down my bare legs. Standing on my toes, balanced with my chest and my cheek and my palms pressed against rotten summer ice. Yelling for someone until my throat is raw, and then swallowing. I like splinting sprained ankles, the sound the tape makes when I rip it. The click when my headlamp turns on. Carrying the litter rail when it is so heavy, the flesh of my fingers flattens and the metal bar reverberates against my bones. And it's a tangible set of steps, literal physical steps, back. All these physical signs mean I'm not worried, I'm being effective. The known is so much less scary than the unknown. The known can usually be accomplished smoothly, deftly, quickly. I like running stuff on the field side better.

I'm headed north. My mom finally answers the phone.

"Mom," I say, "how's it going?" I don't tell her I'm already halfway to her house. "How'd that picture of the crows turn out? Is City Hall going to buy it?" Then I ask casually, disinterestedly, "Any chance you're around today? Vivi says she misses you. . . ."

At one stoplight, I tie my left shoe. At the next one, I tie the right one. Vivian is singing as loudly as she can: *"But then the lifeguard said there'd been nothing to fear. It was nothing but a harmless little dear. Baby shark do doo do do da doo, baby shark."* Over and over. I look in the rear view mirror, and her blond hair is a poufy tangle on one side where she slept on it.

The weather is strange, humid and cool; the steering wheel has an almost imperceptible layer of moisture, but it's enough to cause me to recoil involuntarily when I turn a corner and the wheel slides through my hands. Yesterday we had thunderstorms and inches of hail in the mountains. I haven't looked at the forecast for today.

A lot of people are coming: Seattle, Tacoma, and Everett mountain rescue volunteers, ESAR folks to search nontechnical areas from King, Pierce, and Snohomish counties, Northwest Horseback Search and Rescue, and one of King County's helicopters. Each of the teams has a designated coordinator—SMR's nicknamed our in-town operation leader the ITOL, and the position rotates on a weekly basis, and usually ends up being whoever's on the injured list, or someone who knows they're going to be stuck at work— and they're all communicating, starting to come up with a plan and divvy up assignments by phone. For a big search like this we'll also have someone with a lot of area experience stay in base in order to help with planning, once folks arrive and things start rolling. We'll use our sister units from different counties wherever they can fill in, whenever they're able to get here.

We can't get coordinates from the trail runner's phone; there's no cell phone service anywhere near this area. We can only speculate whether he's somewhere along his route or veered off it at any point in hundreds of square miles. Some parts of his chosen route have no trail; the parts that do start wide and dusty, but as they stretch on mile after mile, farther and farther from civilization, they become indistinct: heather bushes with dark dirt spaced between them in all directions, then slight, angling depressions zigzagging up scree slopes, and finally, rocks and ice over narrow mountain passes. Places that see a lot more marmots than humans.

I drop Vivi off without telling my mom that if we can't find the trail runner today, I will not be picking her up today. Finally I pull into the ranger station in Skykomish, next to Taylor's car. A couple of other folks are here, but it's still pretty quiet.

I never bring camping gear. Missions may last multiple days, but we never really stop moving. It's always more of one continuous push—one long day—until we either find the person we're looking for, or come back in to regroup. At most we sit down with our feet in our packs for a few hours and then start moving again.

I look through my stuff in the back of the car. I have bars, but nothing that can be cooked, and nothing to cook it with. I thought I brought a water purifier, but can't find it now. Hopefully, someone will have iodine tablets. I'm wearing shorts and a T-shirt. I pack pants and a hat, radio, water, headlamp, navigation stuff, med kit, and a trash-compactor bag, and go to find Taylor.

Ten minutes later Taylor, MattyP, and Jonah head up the trail with me. One ESAR team set out ahead of us, and a little before noon, not long after we leave the trailhead, they run into the missing hikers on the Necklace Valley Trail. It's fortunate the hikers found the trail again. The trail runner who made it out said he'd run into these lost hikers the previous day in a bowl south of Tank Lakes. He thought they seemed lost, with no GPS or map, and he tried to explain to them how to get back to the Necklace Valley trail, although he wasn't sure they would remember the turns. But now they're fine, and walking out.

We pass the ESAR team with the hikers, damp with sweat and last night's unanticipated hail, and now coated in a layer of dust. The ESAR team has one SMR member with them.

"Heya, Stephanie," I say, "do you want to keep walking these guys out, or hike back in with us?"

"I'll go with you," she says.

And then we see how much of the missing trail runner's route we can do in daylight. I'm speed walking behind MattyP, the physics teacher from Seattle Prep, who moonlights on ski patrol and takes advantage of his summers off to ramble around the Tetons. He's in his early thirties, and wears trendier clothes than the rest of us. Right now he's talking about his earnest desire to own a VW bus. Taylor's in a quandary because, when he graduates, he's worried that his future workmates will expect him to drive a nice car. His girlfriend is a real estate agent, and she has to have a fairly presentable vehicle, but he doesn't want to let go of his beater Subaru.

Before we left base, we talked to a friend of the missing trail runner who says she thinks he might have found trouble at La Bohn Gap. The other trail runner, the one who came out okay, detoured around this place and Tank Lakes because of snow. The county's helicopter flew over La Bohn Gap, and saw nothing. I think the weather was good enough that if there were anything to see, the helicopter crew would have seen it. Still, it makes sense that this is the place—this is where his friends said to look—and so our plan is to walk the entire route, calling his name, but focus there. We'll be at La Bohn Gap in a little over nine miles.

It's stifling hot and we're walking steeply uphill, not quite running, but fast enough that it hurts like running. I've been out of water for a long time when we cross the outflow of Jewel Lake. A bleached white log bridges the steep descent of frothing, pale-blue water, and we stop to refill our bottles. It turns out that nobody has iodine tablets, but it's too hot not to risk drinking. At a certain point of thirst, I find there is no way I can stop myself, anyway.

We've seen no one else since the overdue hikers. We're just about to start moving again when a trail runner flies past us, heading downhill. We yell after him, and he skids to a stop a little ways below us, keeping his body pointed downhill, just turning his head to look at us.

"I can't stop!" he yells over his shoulder. "I need to report a bad accident. Need to keep running."

We tell him that we're the rescue party, because that is not patently obvious.

"You sure?" he asks.

"We're sure," I say.

He tries to describe the place where the runner is lying, near death after having fallen some distance, but we can't understand. He has a thick Russian accent, and we're talking about turns and valleys and places with no names, using hand gestures. He says he can show us, and we're grateful.

"Hurry," he says, "or he will die before you get there."

I say, "Okay, we'll follow you."

He runs ahead and then keeps running back to admonish us to hurry. After five minutes he takes Stephanie's pack so we can go faster, but I wish that he would take mine instead. Stephanie is faster than I am.

I keep trying to contact base to tell them what we've learned, but we're at the limits of the radio's range. The heat is oppressive and the pace is beyond my aerobic threshold. I'm sucking dirt off the trail and mosquitoes out of the dense, heavy woods, and I can feel it all depositing deep into my lungs, mixing together into the kind of weight that is more emotional than physical. The kind where you watch your friends getting farther and farther away.

Every time I try the radio I have to hold it up in the air, and I can't do that and run uphill with a pack. Taylor turns his head and looks at me; he won't leave me unless I tell him to. I motion for him to go. I can figure out where they went. Probably. We're in a maze of braided meandering mountain goat trails. Taylor and the others are out of sight in seconds.

Standing on stepping stones along the western edge of tiny Opal Lakes, I finally get ahold of base. There are two different command posts now, one in Skykomish and the other at Alpental, and I'm able to contact Alpental. Though the radio's been silent for a long time, suddenly there's constant traffic. I have to wait, trying to break in while someone tries to close a parking lot to make a landing zone for a helicopter, and a horse team, miles and miles away tries checking in and relaying their position. Their radio cuts out and they have to repeat their GPS coordinates several times. I stand on one foot and then the other, looking at the lake next to me, and then the steep, snow-topped scree all around. I am just a cog in the machine, one moving piece among fifty. One piece in a hundred maybe. It's hard to remember this, and wait my turn.

Finally I get through, and base says they'll send the helicopter out, but I need to call back when I reach the runner to give them coordinates. Until then, they'll keep doing what they were doing. And then I'm off again.

Finally I can see La Bohn Gap and my team strung out ahead of me, crossing the last days of a dying glacier, suncups of smooth, clear ice topped with black dirt, and then higher, whiter than the snow, 1,000 feet of loose granite stairs. When I reach them they grate together with a sound like rough glass when I shift my weight. The stairs steepen into a loose scramble up crumbling ten-foot vertical steps, and I'm reaching over my head for the next holds, preferring the granite grouted with black mud and moss to the steep snow patches that link up to the convex, icy summer snow of the Gap still above me.

The trail runner slid from near the top of the Gap. His trekking poles are still 200 feet above where he landed. I trace the slide path, snow newly cleaned, with my finger. The momentum carried him wheeling through the granite blocks, the edges the whitest granite I have ever seen, leaving bloodstains like rose petals. He is at the edge of a small bench above a cliff. Slightly more momentum and he would have fallen another 500 feet. It feels airy, walking the last few feet toward him on the loose granite.

It's clear that, after five minutes, MattyP and Jonah have done everything EMTs can do this far in the backcountry with their med kit and everything in their packs. Jonah is leaning over the runner with his eyes closed, trying to tell if he's still breathing, and MattyP has his hand on Jonah's shoulder.

He must have fallen twenty-four hours ago. He's been lying here unconscious all this time, through the hailstorm, the night, and into this afternoon. I think he's going to die. Right now, actually; it seems clear even from a distance. People do, sometimes, wait to die until someone is with them.

I think about my old job for the private ambulance company. I visited so many long-term care facilities built for people who suffered devastating head injuries and were never going to wake up. It stands out in my mind as one of the worst horrors that can befall a person. The thought flashes through my mind that his injury is too severe for him to regain any of his life; that the kindest thing I can do is hold his hand until he does die.

But just because my hands can't heal bupkis doesn't mean that someone else with more skill can't put this man's life back together. I'm not playing God. I have one job, and that job is to call base. So I call base with our coordinates, and tell them to ask the sheriff's office to launch their helicopter. Maybe someone can fix this. Maybe he just needs the time to fix himself. Maybe he'll die. I cross my fingers and hope it's any one of these.

Deputy Pete winches out of the helicopter. Taylor and I help package, and then Pete winches back up again with the trail runner in his red Bowman bag. For all the world they look the way a rescue is supposed to look: Carried away from certain death by a giant bird, flying through the air suspended by a cable, looking down at Mount Hinman and Silver Eagle and a string of tiny, shimmering alpine lakes. Like in the movies when Superman leaves, we stand watching silently until they're just tiny specks in the distance.

I check my watch; it's 5:30 in the afternoon. As soon as the rotor wash dissipates, the mosquitoes come back. There are dried salt lines on my backpack's black straps, but the back of my shirt is cold with slime. The sun is now lower than the hills, and whatever warmth the solar radiation provided through the clouds is gone. It's a merciful change from the heat, but it's cold. I use my trash-compactor bag to gather used gloves and discarded trauma dressing packages, and crinkle my latest Mylar space blanket into a medium-sized reflective ball. I stuff the garbage into my pack and we start walking the nine miles back.

Months later, I find out the trail runner has made a full recovery. In a small-world kind of way, he's now the main running partner of another SMR volunteer, Andrei, who joined SMR after he broke his back and leg on Guye Peak twenty-seven days after this incident. Now Andrei and I go climbing together at Vertical World on Tuesdays, along with a bunch of other SMR folk. Every week after a few hours in the gym we go to the Black Raven, sit down at our table in the back, and make a toast to life, friendship, and meeting whatever the week is going to bring with integrity. If it's someone's birthday, we also bring cake.

Andrei has convinced me, Russell, Taylor, Larry, and McCall to be real trail runners, which is good because I need to get faster; though sometimes in the middle of a long run, I suddenly realize that I've stopped, and I'm just watching the rain land in the dirt, the force of the water finger-painting the earth with high-gloss swirls, and I let the GPS tracker run on.

THE SLOT AND
THE PHANTOM

IN THE SKI TRIP REPORTS forum on Turns-All-Year.com I'm more of a lurker than a poster, but I keep a screen shot from a post from five years ago. It's an excerpt from a lengthy firsthand account of an avalanche that I responded to. The avalanche injured three skiers in a group of five out for a dawn patrol before work one Wednesday morning in April—all industry professional skiers worth their salt do a lap before work these days. They were caught in an avalanche on the Phantom, a huge old slide path on Mount Snoqualmie created one night in the '90s when it took out a few thousand feet of old-growth forest and the Alpental ski area's maintenance shed at the bottom.

The five skiers had been headed for the Slot Couloir, from high on the west ridge of Mount Snoqualmie it drops down the north side into Thunder Creek Basin, away from Interstate 90 and toward the Middle Fork. The Slot is 40 degrees at its steepest, and narrowish, but not unduly so. It's a bit of a hike to get to the Slot; you go up the Phantom, on the I-90 side across from the ski area, and then down the Slot or one of the other, steeper couloirs. It used to be considered a day trip. Now, when conditions are good, it's part of the dawn-patrol circuit, easy to round-trip before work with an alpine start. People used to run marathons, too, but now marathons are for weenies, and everybody's doing ultras. Keeping up feels exhausting sometimes.

That day, as soon as the five skiers left the parking lot, they saw that conditions were too spicy to ski steeper terrain like the Slot. They were all okay with not skiing it. The crew decided to just skin up the trees at the edge of the Phantom instead. They wanted to get some exercise and look down at the Slot, high on the shoulder of the mountain, and then ski this safer terrain back again.

But they didn't even make it up to look.

Here's the excerpt I keep about the rescue, from one of the injured skiers: "The whole thing felt more like a happy reunion than an unfortunate accident—which, I guess, it kind of was." That part is followed by this: "I was struck by how positive everyone was, how much they were enjoying themselves."

I keep it because it's so incongruous, but so true. It feels slightly wrong to talk about one of the worst days of someone's life as having any sort of upside—but if I can combine being out in the mountains with running into twenty of my best friends, and making any sort of a dent in helping someone out, and if everybody lives to talk about it, well, that is a good day.

It's not just SMR folk, I think, that feel this way. There's something about doing this work that draws people who are inclined toward universal positive regard. One time, Caley's hiking partner broke his leg hiking Silver Peak, across I-90 from Granite Mountain. Caley called 911, but he called us first, so Russ and I ran down Mailbox Peak, headed over, and splinted the guy's leg. KCSO wanted a helicopter, but they had some difficulty finding an available one, so we ended up with a Blackhawk from Fort Lewis. The army medic got stuck in the U-bend of the rope as he rappelled down; one end came out of the helicopter and the other end was stuck up above him in a tall tree. We managed to shake him loose. He was such a cool guy. When his feet were finally on the ground, he came over with a massive smile and started fist-bumping everyone and yelling, "Hello, Brother!" He made a person feel good.

After the army medic flew off with Caley's hiking partner we were hungry. It was so late that it was early when we finally sat down at the North Bend Bar and Grill. It was more crowed than usual, and I couldn't remember seeing so many children there before, but thankfully our usual table was open. Our usual waiter tactfully opened a window behind us. I ordered a beer and then the waiter mentioned they were serving brunch now, so I had pancakes too, and I sat there looking over my beer and pancakes at the rest of the table of gaunt, bleary-eyed crew, and it was a perfect moment of bliss. Unfortunately, I was wrecked after one beer and a full stack of pancakes with two of those little plastic containers of syrup, and I had to sleep in my car for three hours, but it was worth it.

The avalanche that caught the five skiers happened around 9:45 in the morning, high on Mount Snoqualmie, just below the entrance to the Slot. The two uninjured skiers called 911, but first they called their backcountry professional ski buddies to help bail them out. I can't fault them for that.

The helicopter couldn't come because of strong, gusty winds, even in the parking lot at Alpental, and it was snowing thick and fast. Russell went in first to figure out the safest way to locate the skiers and put a track in, since so much snow was coming down that all their tracks had been covered over. We divvied up the crew between the two of us. He got a paramedic skier from Everett, an Alpental Pro Patroller, the hard-core ski buddies, and a backpack full of medical supplies, and then they skied off, because skiing is the only way to get anywhere in the backcountry, and because the skiing was phenomenal.

I got Aaron, who had blown off another day of med school to be here; I was surprised the UW hadn't kicked him out yet.

"Aaron," I asked, "how do you do it?"

"You know what they call a doctor who graduates last in his class?" Aaron asked.

"Doctor," said Jonah from behind me.

"There it is!" shouted Aaron joyfully, rubbing his hands together. "What do you want me to carry?"

We had all the gear we needed to get the skiers back out, litters, ropes, and hardware. The rest of the crew came with me to help hump gear.

We took snowshoes, because even though snowshoes are an accursed method of travel, it is easier to carry insane loads with them, and they make for faster maneuvering around trees while making anchors, and lowering a litter through terrain too steep and cliffy for tobogganing. Traveling anywhere in snowshoes takes so much more effort, though, and I feel like a dork when I'm wearing them, because backcountry skiers spend an inordinate amount of time dissing on snowshoers. Being a snowshoer is just not cool. Jenn, who is better at staying up on these sorts of issues than I am, tells me that brown is the new black, purple is the new pink, and I'm not allowed to wear gaiters, even in knee-deep slush, because it would be a huge fashion faux pas.

"No one in Colorado wears gaiters," she tells me.

"How often do they have knee-deep slush there?" I ask her.

"You're totally missing the point!"

Her voice echoed in my head, even though she was at work fifty miles away. I sensed without even having to be told that wearing snowshoes was worse than wearing gaiters.

Usually, the key to snowshoe travel is to expend a lot more effort to try to match pace with the skiers, but we were being careful that day. Just because Russ's crew had gone this way didn't mean that we were willing to follow his track without looking at it ourselves.

"Team 2, Team 1," Russell called over the radio.

"Team 2," I answered, still slogging forward.

"I'm with the party now," said Russ. "We're going to head up toward the crown of the avalanche. There's a guy up there with a possible femur fracture with a ski pole traction splint. There's another guy about 250 feet lower with injured knees. You take that one. Then there's a third guy. He's up and moving around, but he lost his skis. He can walk out but he needs snowshoes." Russ wanted everybody but me and Aaron to keep going up to where he was, bringing most of the gear we had, so he could start extracting the upper guy as soon as possible.

I called the SMR's ITOL, and asked him to call our roster, along with Everett and Tacoma mountain rescues', so I could get some more people headed my way.

The temperature was in the mid-20s, and windy. It was still dumping snow, with over two feet of new, and because of wind deposition some sections were up to waist-deep, all of it falling over mushy rain-soaked snow. If I wasn't already jumpy enough about the potential for wind slabs—where a well-bonded dense snow layer sitting on top of less consolidated well-lubricated snow can suddenly crack off and slide in chunks—the idea of going to get some guys who just got caught in one that ran over a thousand feet made me jumpier.

But I have to admit to myself that seeing the consequences of one person after another being crushed in avalanches gives me an inaccurate perspective of risk. I know intellectually that so much success, so much joy and fulfillment comes with spending time in the mountains. Sunny days and champagne powder, exhilaration in many forms. Thousands of guys meeting thousands of large-breasted girls in ski lodges for après. First descents. Feats of quick thinking and unreal athleticism combining into Zen flight in chutes, over cliffs, and down huge, beautiful, and remote mountains on seven continents. I know it's out there. Folks leading brilliant lives in the strong, reflected sunshine. Risk and reward. But nobody calls me for that. And I don't even do that much brilliant sunshine skiing on my own time, either.

I mean I do it, but I'm drawn to the silence. To obscure places. To little streams that still run, ink-black ribbons, slick exposed rocks topped with plush, extravagant, blinding white. I like the crack of tree limbs in the cold. I like . . . I can't deny it. I like skiing ice. Ice over cliffs and between crevasses in whiteout conditions. Old icy tree bombs frozen over with lichen and tree duff in thick woods, dry dead branches tearing at my clothes, snapping, and I like the pain of the scratches. I like being the only bright spot where no moonlight filters through the canopy, tearing through the night. Maybe I misunderstand what attracts most people to skiing. Maybe I don't understand the reward part how I'm supposed to.

But this was my favorite kind of rescue. Most of the others were huddled around the guy with the broken femur, just far enough away to be out of earshot. It was a beautiful place. Snow is so intoxicating, such a tactile experience, tickling my nose, landing in my eyelashes, siding in a flat, white, smooth shear as I pulled my shovel forward, testing the snow, and I could feel each individual hair raise on the back of my neck. I couldn't help it. A touch of anxiety causes hyper-awareness, makes me better at everything. I could smell the massive grey trees around us, hung with waving, brilliant-lime lichen. I switched back and forth between listening to Aaron talking to the skier while checking out his knees—"So, clotheslined basically. Cheese and rice, dude!"—and then listening to each individual wind-driven snowflake as it reverberated onto the stiff fabric of my jacket.

A bit later, Oyvind showed up to help us, with a guy named Pie from EMRU. He was wearing a helmet that said PIE in all capital letters. Oyvind saw me looking dubious, and leaned over the litter toward me as we burritoed the skier in a blue 9x12 tarp.

Rolling his eyes, he whispered, "He was homeschooled."

"So was I," I whispered back.

Oyvind shook his head and groaned, and I grinned and wrinkled my nose. Behind us, Aaron exploded with laughter, still talking to the injured skier. "Okay, but how did you get the smell out?" I had no idea what he was talking about, but Aaron has always been good at building rapport.

Then we were off.

It wasn't exactly a race back down the 2,800 feet to Alpental, but, in the best interest of getting our guy to definitive care, we weren't dawdling. Russ had almost all of the manpower and most of the gear up with the skier with the broken femur, but we managed to cobble some stuff together. We had to lower a fair bit, which is onerous, and without a rigging kit we were wrapping the rope around trees, winding and unwinding to change the friction. But it worked out. The snow was pretty deep and created a lot of drag, and as I got more and more people, I tied all the webbing we had to the back of the litter. Two guys in front were pulling forward to steer, and then I had ten snowshoers from ESAR sit down with their feet in front of them digging into the snow, acting as human anchors, all being dragged along at about three miles an hour. It looked pretty hilarious and unprofessional, and I'm sure they got a lot of snow down their pants, and I'm sorry about that, but it worked—until we got to a steeper slope.

I overestimated the power of the drag and the whole crew rocketed off, leaving Aaron and me at the top of the rise, peering over.

I worried it would end badly, but even after I lost sight of them, I could hear whooping and laughter, and they didn't hit anything, so I realized that I'd underestimated their sledding skills. I caught up with them again once the slope eased, following the wavy line of butt prints in the snow, and we made it back to Alpental and the waiting aid cars a full half hour before Russ's crew. Aaron and I were undeniably proud because it was probably the first time in history, anywhere in the world, that a group of snowshoers beat a group of skiers at anything.

"What hospital do you want to go to?" Aaron asked the skier. "I need to let the ambulance crew know where to take you."

"No, thanks," said the skier, "I'll just hang here until my buddies get out, and then they can load me in the Subie."

Both Aaron and I spent some time, long ago, driving for private ambulance companies, and we both understand the dirtbag lifestyle heralded by both climbers and skiers. Aaron still lived it. He told me as we were walking across the parking lot that right now he was living on nothing but fifty-pound bags of potatoes—the cheapest food in the grocery store—topped with condiment packets scrounged from fast-food establishments.

We did tell this skier that we thought he should take the ambulance ride, even though it costs money, because getting strained through trees for five hundred feet at a high rate of speed can sometimes cause other, more life-threatening injuries that only present themselves further down the line.

"You feel okay," said Aaron, "and then, suddenly, BAM, you're dead."

But I had to respect that this skier was a professional, a much more hard-core climber and skier than I would ever be, and hard climbers and skiers cling to independence and—climbers anyway—to cheapness with a ferocity that transcends pain. Or maybe they love the pain. Anyway, he could not be persuaded to take the ambulance.

So we told him to call 911 again if anything changed, swapped the litter, which we needed to keep, for a backboard to keep his legs splinted together, and figured out a way to jam him in between the hatchback rail and the rear window of his friend's Subaru. In a time-honored tradition, we explained to his carpool buddy our accident-related tribal knowledge of how to drive up on the ambulance-only ramp at Harborview, and then explained how he needed to wave his arms in front of the locked emergency room door so the security guards would see him. We demonstrated proper waving technique. After that, they were on their own.

I don't know how to define wilderness. Maybe the Phantom is still a wild place even though it can be accessed in only a few hours from a major freeway? Maybe now that it's just a dawn patrol, just done for exercise, it has lost some of its wildness. Sidecountry to a freeway, where rescue comes in a few hours. It's white bread, I suppose, compared to real mountains, but there is still something that keeps me here, beholden to this place, to the people who love it most. Maybe this is why I like skiing at night, when it still feels like what it is: an ancient range of mountains, obscured from view in powerful, thick fog.

Time went by, and then it was a midmorning in January, with fog blowing in and out. I was in the middle of an avalanche class I was taking with a bunch of other SMR folks, digging a test pit about 500 feet below the exit notch for the Slot—the way back up to regain the ridge after skiing down the couloir—when we got a call for a man with a broken leg at the bottom of the Slot. The man had been skiing with his wife. She was wearing a helmet. She fell and rocketed head-first into his leg. The leg broke. We skied over.

We splinted the leg with a ski pole and a shovel handle. I was standing next to Martin, the owner of Pro Ski and Guiding in North Bend, and an IFMGA guide from Switzerland. He'd been teaching our class, so we brought him along with us.

"We have to get a helicopter," said Martin. He kept repeating it over and over because it would be a nightmare to try to carry some-one out from the bottom of the Slot. Impossible, maybe.

"It would be tough," I said, "but if the fog gets any thicker, I guess we'll figure it out." Russ and six of the other fastest SMR guys had just skied all the way down the Phantom to pick up the gear from our truck in the parking lot at Alpental, and as we were talking they were skinning back up again.

But just as I was wondering if Russ had called his mom from the parking lot while he had cell phone service, to make sure she could

keep watching Vivi, the fog cleared briefly, and the helicopter managed to winch down a sheriff's deputy and nab the injured man. They
were off, just as the fog closed back in. Two seconds later, we were
standing there alone with our hands in our pockets, partially frozen
and all covered with rotor-wash-driven snow.

Another party skiing down the Slot kindly picked up all the wife's
ski gear. Once we got her sorted out—she was a little gun-shy about
skiing again—we skied out with her, and then we went to the North
Bend Bar and Grill for dinner. In order to get enough space we dis-
placed a small family and pushed all the tables together in our usual
corner. It's a spectacle, when we come together there. I like seeing my
friends packed together like so many pieces of my heart. It only works
with all the pieces. Ryan wanted to raise a glass, but he didn't want to
say why, just led a toast in silence, and I took a picture of everyone's
arms raised together, trying not to spill Mac and Jack's Cascadian
Dark on our deep-fried jalapeños. Then Russ and I headed home,
stopping on the way to pick up Vivi and her round pink suitcase.

But after Martin's Swiss Mountain Guide doubts that we could
pull someone out of the Slot, it seemed both like it was inevitable,
and also that it was on, just a little bit. If we did it, we'd have to stop
by his shop in North Bend and tell him about it. See if he'd give us a
discount on a hat, or something.

When it comes, the trouble is that the timing's inconvenient. The
next text for a skier in the Slot with two broken legs arrives on a
Sunday afternoon when we've already spent all of the day before
and all that morning doing a rope-rescue training, utterly drenched
and half-frozen, practicing using ropes to float people over the tops
of moss-covered cliffs and scree slopes in the woods just below snow
line. We're two hours from wrapping up the seminar, and heading
to the North Bend Bar and Grill for Jalisco chicken burgers. Jenn
has just discovered that in addition to the deep-fried jalapeños they
also serve deep-fried pickles, and I'm excited to try them. Paramedic
school has been taking up a lot of time, and I haven't been around
much, so I was looking forward to dinner with everyone, before we
got the call.

Looking up at the flat grey North Bend sky, and down at the
deepening river of rain on the trail as we jogged out, humping our

300-foot 11-mil static lines, our rope gun, and half the hillside's worth of mud, I can tell that the helicopter isn't going to pull off this rescue. There's a blizzard at Snoqualmie Pass.

The worst part is that we don't have our skis. If I left my skis on the roof rack at any trailhead, they'd be stolen before I got back. It feels risky enough to keep my avi and SAR gear in a duffle out of sight in the car. So the skis are at home.

Up at the pass, Randy from the volunteer ski patrol hands me, with a flourish, a blue plastic tub full of snowshoes he's scrounged up for us.

"Thanks for the loan, Randy," I say.

"Nobody's used these puppies in ages. Might want to check 'em before you start out."

I'm grateful. But I still hate snowshoes. I hand them out, and it's like being the bearer of bad news to dangle them in front of Russ, McCall, Larry, Caley, Jenn, and the rest of the guys that we convinced to give up dinner with friends for a mad snowshoe sprint into darkness. Some of them are MSRs from about ten years ago, which isn't too bad, and some of them are a bit older than that.

"Hmm," says McCall, "spruce and rawhide. Holy shit. I get to play Clint Eastwood."

There's cloud cover with a 7,000-foot ceiling. The sheriff's office called in some deputies for overtime and put the helicopter on standby at the hangar in Seattle, just in case things improve despite the weather report. But the report seems pretty accurate: thick fog and flat, flying snowflakes everywhere, and it's only supposed to dump more snow into the evening. Two ski patrol volunteers, Andy and Troy, along with one of SMR's doctors, Dr. Fergie, were up at the Pass already, and they have almost an hour's head start on us. While it's still daylight, they manage to dig some hasty avalanche test pits, call down conditions reports, and spend the time to put in the safest route. They call down to us that it's slow going.

Russ wants to meet them at the exit notch, and he feels we can catch them, even with the snowshoes, so Russ, Larry, and I set off, still carrying the ropes, twenty pounds each when they're dry, but now sodden and heavier than that, along with a bunch of gear from the rigging training, and warming and medical gear. The rest of the guys are just behind us, carrying even more gear. We are all instantly covered in a layer of snow that melts into a familiar dampness at the edges of our hats.

This is an aerobic activity, so I strip down to a T-shirt and roll my pants up to my knees. The snow melts instantly on my arms and the back of my neck, running all the way down into my boots. It's not painful exactly, keeping up. Folks always compare things to childbirth, and I birthed Vivian after thirty-eight hours of unmedicated back labor, so I feel qualified to make the comparison. I think giving birth is hard because there is nothing you can do to make it stop, even when you need a break; you can't slow a new life from entering the world even if the effort rips you in half. But this is a conscious effort, my brain screaming at me to stop. It's all about maintaining focus despite the initial agony, and later deadening.

It's hard to read the snowpack, hard to maintain speed, make good decisions, communicate concerns, and make a plan when I don't have the breath to do it; don't have enough oxygen to concentrate. It's a wild dance; the faster we go, the less likely some hypothermic guy we've never met with two broken legs will die in the middle of a snowy chute on the back side of a random mountain. But I need to be able to think, too. It's a weird predicament.

We pass Fergie, white hair sticking out from under his newsboy cap, skinning up the track Troy put in. We pass him and meet up with Troy at the exit notch where there is now only 200-foot visibility because of snow, ice fog, and 40-knot wind gusts. Base says the forecast is calling for decreasing visibility, increasing winds, and more snow.

We stop for a second to talk about what to do. We'll lose radio contact with base as soon as we drop down the backside of the exit notch.

Russ says, "Caley will be here in a few minutes, I can focus on what we need to do to get the skier from the bottom of the Slot across the basin to the bottom of the Notch and then back up to here. Larry can assign jobs to the rest of the teams when they come in and figure out how to get the skier from the Notch back down the Phantom."

Troy says, "Andy's already dropped down the Notch and is trying to make his way over to the skier."

"Okay," says Russ. "Bree can follow him down and do medical until Fergie gets there. That'll free Andy up to keep doing snow assessment."

I look briefly down, contemplating the slope, the aspect, the pitfalls of steep downhill snowshoeing. I roll my pants back down while Troy's a few steps ahead of me, trying to see if he can ski cut anything. But nothing's moving; the storm layers from early in the week are pretty consolidated and well-bonded. Troy says he'll keep an eye on me from below in the basin, with Russ and Larry watching from the top in case it does slide while I'm on it. Once Troy is down I take off, following his and Andy's ski track, trying not to be jealous of their turns as I'm miring up to mid-thigh on one sunken snowshoe and then the other, struggling out and miring again, always with the same power pushing forward, whether my feet can move or not. It's just about continuing to move and consistently thinking light, stable thoughts.

Andy calls over the radio, "Watch the other chutes between the Notch and the Slot. They're all a similar aspect."

"Okay," I radio back. "We're not taking a direct line to the base of the Slot, we're dropping down lower into the basin, around any potential avalanche run-out zones." At least, we think we're dropping low enough, based on how far we're guessing a potential slide might run into the basin.

When I find the skier I see that it's a lot worse than two broken legs. Around 11 a.m. the skier and his partner triggered a six-inch soft wind slab which broke wall to wall at the chute's choke point, churning him for a thousand feet to the confluence of the Crooked and Slot couloirs. At the end, his feet and legs were caught fast but his upper body was pushed along by the snow, bending and crushing him under its weight. When the snow stopped, the skier was flattened but only partially buried. His partner dug him the rest of the way out, and then he struggled back up to the Notch in order to get cell phone service; he'd finally been able to connect with 911 around noon.

It's already three in the afternoon when I get there. The first five or ten minutes are easy. I can tell from five feet away whether or not someone's in danger of imminent death. I can do a primary assessment—check to see if he's conscious and breathing, look for blood. I can take vital signs, try to ask some pertinent questions. I can do a pretty decent detailed assessment, although I'm hesitant to expose very much skin. When I lift his shirt up, the wind instantly blows it full of snow. I'm pretty good at stabilizing any bone a human being can fracture.

But the reporting party was wrong when he said that this rescue was going to be about two broken legs. I don't have that much useful kit—no drugs or fluids, and anyway at a certain point nobody but a surgeon can fix multisystem trauma. So after five or ten minutes using all the actual skills and equipment I have, I'm stuck just waiting for the litter to show up. I don't have anything left for my hands to do. Then it's just me and Andy, on our knees next to the man, waiting for Fergie, waiting for Caley, Russell, and Larry to move the gear and the people into position so we can blow this pop stand. But they're going to have to do it fast.

The skier's partner, along with a good Samaritan—a former Mount Baker Pro Patroller—have been doing jumping jacks to stay warm for hours already, but it's too cold to stand around for as long as they have. The Good Samaritan says he's cold, and I give him my warm synthetic pumpkin jacket and put my shell back on over my T-shirt. Fergie shows up with his med bag.

"Hey Ferg," I say, "Here's the deal—"

After my fifteen-second explanation of the man's condition, Fergie says, "Stay here and help me for a bit."

"You got it," I tell him.

With each additional person who crests the Notch, more equipment arrives: the litter, heat packs, and sleeping bags. Andy's putting the litter's two halves together, lining it with a tarp and sleeping bags. All together, we lift the man into the litter, trying to keep out as much snow as we can. We're keeping it organized, almost ready to move.

When I look up again, Andy motions that he wants to talk to me. "I don't want to go out under the chutes," he says. The side-hill skin track the skier's partner put in under the chutes earlier in the day is the shortest line back to the Notch, but even avalanche hazard aside, side-hilling while carrying a litter is nightmarish. It's too steep for folks to walk next to the litter; we'd have to put in anchors to keep everybody from sliding downhill.

"Okay, let's go down into the basin, and then back up to the Notch," I say.

Andy and I nod at each other and wheel around to keep working.

After another minute, Fergie stands up and motions that he wants to talk to me. "I think he's going to die before we get out," whispers Fergie, not looking at me, but out to where the basin would be if he could see it in the worsening visibility. "How fast can you guys get him out of here?"

I don't look at Fergie either, but at the basin, feeling the cold pressing into my back. I'm already shivering pretty hard. Now I can only see maybe fifty feet because of the freezing fog, which is everywhere and seemingly undeterred by the wind. It's going to be dark really soon. It is a long way back to Alpental.

"This is a good team," I tell Ferg, "but it's a long way. Tell him not to die."

"I know," he says.

Fergie relays to Larry on the radio to tell base to send up as many oxygen bottles as they can get their hands on. We tie webbing onto the litter rails and sled the litter down into the valley, 800 vertical feet, as quickly as we can while pushing through hip-deep snow.

Crossing the basin is onerous. Russ needs me to move the man to the bottom of the Notch, and I tell Fergie I'm going to start rigging. Even though it's nearly flat, there's no bottom to the snow, no purchase to pull from. We end up using skis for anchors and rigging a haul system with Andy's emergency 30-meter 8-mil rope just to get across the flats. But the rope is so skinny, it's like a bungee cord. The litter is barely moving—we're just pulling the stretch out of the rope.

Our 300-foot static ropes are occupied in a haul system waiting for us to get to the bottom of the Notch, but we call up to see if we can get them dropped down in the basin.

"If we drop them, can we get them back up to the Notch again?" Caley radios back, which is a valid point, but our progress has been marked by inches with maximal effort, and every time I look back from digging anchor points or hauling with all my body weight on the rope I can see Fergie down with the litter, waving his arms at me, like, "What the fuck?!"

I key the mike. "We need them down here."

"Drop them," says Russ.

"Done," says Caley, and he and Larry drop the ropes down. That gets us back across the basin with just a couple more anchors, and what would have taken us hours takes only a few minutes, but then, yeah, we have to get the ropes back up to the top of the Notch so they can pull us out of the basin. There are more ropes headed up the Phantom, on the backs of every available SAR person in three counties, but it'll take too long for them to reach us. Shit. I can't remember a time I needed more than 600 feet of rope. I guess now I know of a spot that needs twice that.

"Fergie, Bree," calls Fergie over the radio. He is done with arm waving.

"Go ahead," I say.

"We have to get off this slope. Right now. He can't breathe at this angle."

I look up and it's 640 more feet of steeply angled terrain back up to the Notch. We have to get the ropes up there before they can pull the skier up. Until then he's stuck. "I hear you," I say.

Skis, snowshoes, it doesn't matter. It's a wallow fest. The snow is too steep and shredded, there's no putting a skin track in, and the snowshoes are useless. It's faster to boot it, but the steps collapse one into another and the snow is up to my chest.

I'm next to Bob and Jenn, working the last haul in the basin. "The skier is going to die in the basin in the next few minutes unless you can get the rope up to the Notch," I tell them. I hate saying it because, if he does die, then they'll always feel like maybe somehow they could have done it faster, when the truth is that I know everyone is doing the best they can. But I want them to know why they have to pull it out, right now.

Jenn closes her eyes and takes a deep breath, and says nothing to me, and I realize I've gone too far.

"Ride the lightning!" I scream up at her. My paramedic school instructor just yelled this at me during advanced cardiac life-support training two days before, and I also like thrash metal. At least, I feel like there is a time and place for Metallica. After class I looked up what "ride the lighting" actually means in the Urban Dictionary. It means, "a fuck-it-all attitude. . . . adapt and let yourself go to arbitrary circumstance no matter how austere or violent." Fantastic. Jenn prefers bands that sing about science so she can book them for the library, like Mikey Mike and his socks-and-sandals classic, "Likin' the Lichen."

She looks at me very seriously and extends her index and little finger. Bob starts post-holing, scooping the snow away with his hands to be able to get his knees high enough to take the next step. I hear him gasping for breath as he works his way forward, and Jenn grabs the ends of the ropes and ties them around her waist, dragging them behind her, following in Bob's footsteps. Jenn weighs a hundred pounds soaking wet, which she is right now. I'm not sure if the snow-encrusted ropes weigh more than she does, but I'm sure it's close.

My arms are on fire. I don't have enough people to haul, now that Bob and Jenn are gone, but I have to get the litter up to where I am in order for Jenn to have enough rope left to get to the top, and I do, barely. About a minute later, Jenn and Bob make it to the top. They start the haul, and I realize several things: first, they can't actually see us because of the fog; second, they're in a hurry; third, I am on the wrong side of the rope, digging out someone's skis that I'd been using as anchor material, and the rope is about to catch me as it comes into plumb line.

While it is painful to get launched through the air by a rope snapping tight with the force of a great number of your friends pulling on it, I am grateful that it gets me twenty feet farther uphill. The skier in the litter slides forward, smoothly, quickly, and crests the top of the Notch in seconds.

That leaves me behind Fergie, and we struggled together in the line of folks following the litter.

"I'm so old," gasps Fergie, steadying himself after a wind gust grabs at the skis on his back, threatening to pull him off the slope.

"You're the youngest doctor out here today," I say, pushing up with my shoulder under his butt. "Showing up is half the battle."

I can hear him mutter under his breath, "It's the other half that's the problem."

It feels like victory to get to the top of the Notch, but then I look around and we are still in the middle of the wilderness, a fair shake away from the parking lot. The general atmosphere feels blizzard-like, snow blowing sideways, cold, dark. Easier to see while wearing goggles.

A couple guys from the volunteer ski patrol are able to toboggan the skier down some parts of the Phantom, but we have to lower him down a lot of it, transitioning back and forth with completely frozen hands.

Our runners start to show up with more oxygen bottles, which is good because we've burned through all we had. Halfway down the Phantom, and nearly thirteen hours after the accident, more folks from Everett and Tacoma Mountain Rescue show up to help, and they put together an escort for a paramedic from Medic 1 and march him in on snowshoes carrying more pain meds, among other things.

The skier is still alive when we see the fuzzy yellow lights of Alpental below us. Not only can I not feel my fingers anymore, but I can't feel the skin on my arms, either, and I've given up on trying to wipe at the snot running down my face. It's one in the morning, and I'm starting to stumble. I know what Fergie means when he says he's getting old. I'm grateful just to be done.

The paramedic takes the skier to Harborview. Someone throws down a blue tarp under a pole light over six inches of slush in the parking lot, and everyone starts piling group gear out on it. We are fifty people from six different groups, and all of the gear is soaking wet and half-frozen; our stuff also has a layer of mud from yesterday's training.

"I'm going to take our gear home with me and dry it in my laundry room," says Caley. "It'll never dry out in SMR-1. This is beyond the capabilities of the wonky space heater and dehumidifier combo."

Taking the gear home means that if another rescue comes up tonight, he'll have to go on it, dragging all our stuff with him. We always have to have our shit together, sorted and ready to go, that's what being on call all the time means. But we don't have a building, and nobody can kneel in the snow anymore trying to sort metal 'biners from grey slushballs, or untie frozen knots encased in ice with frozen hands. Or maybe we could, but it feels like it's just too much.

Driving home, I try to remember when I ate last, and I think it was breakfast yesterday. I pull out a bar from the glove box and think about eating it, but I'm not really hungry. I can hear another text beeping, though, and I'm upset. It's too soon to go out again. I want to go home and take a shower first. At least pull some fresh clothes out of the dryer. But when I look down at my phone, it's Larry: "Stopping by Pro Ski tomorrow to buy a hat from Martin."

DOUBLE PEAK
AND OWYHIGH
LAKES

I DON'T TAKE A LOT of vacations. Mostly because, right now, I'm trying to focus on feeling comfortable in my house. I was a climbing bum for a long time, living out of vehicles and crashing on couches. It's only recently that I've stopped waking up in the middle of the night, homesick, and had to get out of bed and go sit in the driver's seat of my car in order to sleep. I don't want to undermine my progress.

Also, the last time I went on vacation was to Whistler for a long weekend with Russell. While we were gone, someone jumped over Snoqualmie Falls. The recovery happened on a freezing midwinter night, even though that's pretty dangerous. There were extenuating circumstances, so it made sense, but four people ended up getting lowered down to the bottom of the falls before it was over, and they got stuck down there, buffeted in the suffocating spray for a long time. One of them also got hit by a rock, and ended up in the hospital. I would rather have been there to help out my friends than watch the texts roll through. Every trip since then has felt slightly furtive.

I know the crew are totally fine without me. In my absence, I'd trust my team with my mother—the fire department tells me that's the gold standard for trust. But there have just been so many times on one rescue or another when I needed someone to have my back, and was so grateful when Caley or McCall or Taylor or Garth came when I asked for more help. I know whenever someone doesn't respond to the initial page, it means they're already busy with something important. So if I keep asking, and then they show up, it means they just ran out of some meeting with their boss, or stuck the fruit salad back in the fridge and bailed on their grandma's ninetieth birthday party. Coming each time our arms are about to give out or we run out of gear is a gift of time, effort, and sacrifice. I'm always really conscious of the times when I'm not in a position to return the favor.

Aaron and I had a deal where, if one of us called then the other one would come, no matter what. I think that made me braver sometimes, when I was out there by myself and had a big job to do. But Aaron's gone. After finishing med school, he got a residency in Portland and moved, and joined Portland Mountain Rescue.

He'd been skiing up the south side of Mount Hood when a climber near him fell and slid into a fumarole. Aaron said that he knew he shouldn't go into the fumarole, for so many reasons, but in the end he said that even if he died trying to get the climber out, he wouldn't be able to live with himself if he didn't try. He ended up with some steam burns, but he got the climber out and neither of them died—which was a little bit lucky, I guess.

PMR put together a committee meeting to decide if they were going to kick Aaron out for being reckless. Before the date of the meeting, Aaron went hiking with his girlfriend, and she dared him to jump into a pool below one of the waterfalls in the Columbia Gorge. So he did it, but he misjudged the distance, hit a submerged rock, and jammed his lower legs up through his knees. His girlfriend went for help. Aaron dragged himself back out of the water and started to crawl because he didn't want PMR to come pick him up, feeling that having to be rescued by them might negatively influence the committee.

Eventually, an off-duty security guard ran across him—actually, appeared above him with his gun drawn, which Aaron said was more disconcerting than anything. But then the security guard explained that he had found Aaron because he was following a trail of blood and drag marks, and Aaron felt that his having the gun out as a precaution was understandable, considering.

Later, the security guard visited Aaron in the hospital and brought him a bottle of vodka. PMR voted to kick Aaron out for being reckless. Aaron wasn't going to really ever be able to climb again, anyway. I told him to drink the vodka.

But I miss having a reckless friend who will do anything to help even a stranger. I know what he would do for me.

In June I was going to take a vacation, and not like the day trips I took once or twice a week with Russell, Larry, and Taylor. I bring Samoas on those trips because Vivian's a Girl Scout, but we rarely get to eat them—those days are about constant movement, never stopping for lunch, always seeing how far we can go. We have to be home by Sunday night; there's always a rescue on Sunday nights. But this time Jenn had a week off from the library, so we were going to drive down to Yosemite and work on our tick list.

I had a little time on my hands again. During paramedic school, my life had been briefly packed with commutes to Tacoma for school, clinicals at night, and forty-eight-hour ride-alongs in Wenatchee almost every weekend. But I left halfway through for a fire fighter job with the City of Bellevue. Even in school I'd never stopped applying for fire department jobs. It's almost impossible to work as a paramedic in King County without being a fire fighter first, and I can never move to another county because Russell's job is better than mine. And my friends and my parents are here. My life is here.

So I left school for the job, but on the first morning of recruit academy, one of the instructors looked me up and down and let me know that it probably wasn't going to work out. And also that I needed to cut my hair to less than three inches. So I did that, but knowing that I was only coming so they could document me doing enough things wrong to make sure I would fail was mentally so much harder than any of the CrossFit. It was about as hard as looking at myself in the mirror each morning.

When they finally got around to telling me officially, near the end of the academy, that they were going to fire me if I didn't quit, the captain told me I should be proud because I was the last woman in the class to be forced to quit or be fired; women almost never make it as far as I did.

I'm not sure why he mentioned it, though; we both knew it wasn't because I was a woman that I wasn't good enough. The department has a couple of women, so women can do it. It was just that the guys in my class were stronger, and it didn't seem like I had a lot of experience throwing ladders and using power tools. There's no real set standard, but it was obvious to everyone. There was a three-inch pile of documentation I could look through if I wanted. I said it was okay, I didn't want to read it.

Russ thought maybe I just hadn't tried hard enough because if you work hard, you succeed. Near the end of my time in the academy, I'd gotten a Norwalk-like virus with horrible diarrhea and vomiting. I went to work anyway, because there was no calling in sick. During one of the morning runs I had diarrhea seeping down my legs, but I kept running for miles, wondering what would happen if I gave it up and squatted in a meticulously landscaped downtown Bellevue median in front of everyone.

So here I am again, and it's June. I got reaccepted into paramedic school, and I'm supposed to start over in the fall. At night, sitting at my desk, I know I need to start applying to more fire departments. I say aloud to myself, "Suck it up, Buttercup. Reinvent yourself. Become better. Become undeniable." But it sounds hollow when I say it. My voice sounds tired, taunting, scared. I know better than to think it just takes hard work to win.

I feel homely—very short hair doesn't suit me. Waiting for my hair to grow back. Waiting to start again. Everyone starts at the bottom, and they have to prove they're worth something, try again to earn the right to respect. But this summer feels like a stay of execution. I can spend one more summer with Vivi before school starts again, and I know volunteer work is not what I should be focusing on right now. But I think there will never be another time in my life when I'll feel more like I'm where I need to be, doing what I want to do.

I kinda just want to stay at home, but Jenn tells me that I need to go on a vacation, get away from everything. It'll be like pushing a big red restart button, she says. I'll come back stronger, refreshed, ready.

"It'll be so relaxing," she says, and at first I'm a little resistant, because I've never had a relaxing vacation.

"Jenn, I say, "I can count on one hand the number of vacations I've taken where I didn't spend the majority of the time cold, hungry, and scared."

"This one will be awesome," says Jenn. "We'll even take lunch breaks."

We're leaving tomorrow morning, and the only thing I have left to do is borrow some gear from Gene at The Mountaineers Program Center, and then go home and pack it.

Jenn knows Gene better than I do, thinks of him as a father figure; he taught her how to climb. I don't belong to the Mountaineers, but Jenn does. Though she tells me that it isn't the dating pool she initially hoped it would be.

"It is too," I tell her. "It's just that you're choosing trips with guys in their seventies, because then your woman-and-her-dog footloose-and-fancy-free lifestyle is safe."

Jenn thinks about this.

"Maybe," she admits, and adds, "friends are just better."

Gene has been Chair of the Mountaineers climbing committee for a long time, but more than that he's built much of the community that keeps the Mountaineers going. He's also been instrumental in getting them into their building at Magnuson Park in Seattle, which I think is very lovely, especially since I come from an organization that has no home at all.

Longer ago, Gene was in SMR, but he left soon after I joined—he's seventy-five now—so we know each other, but we aren't close. I know of that old-timey SMR crew, some of their stories, and how hard core they were.

I always think of Dave, one of Gene's contemporaries that I knew best. A few years ago, in January, a snowshoer went missing in the Middle Fork of the Snoqualmie River in a storm. Russ and I were out looking for her near Lower Tuscohatchie Lake. It was bone-achingly cold and blowing rain. At the same time, Dave and Steve the engineer were trying to work their way up toward us, but Dave slipped on the slushy bank of a raging stream cascading down toward the Middle Fork, and fell in. It was dark by then, and Dave was completely submerged. Steve said he could see Dave's headlamp still glowing underwater, heading downstream fast. The water rushes through there, between rocks and over drop after drop down the valley. Steve started running down the bank, all the while keeping an eye on the light, while Dave tried to grab one slimy, snow-topped rock after another. He could grab them for a minute, but then the water dragged him on again. Finally, Steve got to a spot with an overhanging log. He dove out onto it, reached down, grabbed Dave, and hauled him out. Dave stripped naked, wrung out his wool pants, dried himself with snow, and they kept going. Dave must have been at least seventy years old at the time. The snowshoer we were looking was for found three days later, exhausted and wearing a pair of huge, yellow plastic rain pants she found in an abandoned hunter's camp. She said she knew she was hallucinating, but she thought maybe she'd been led there by a Native American apparition. That's neither here nor there, but that's how gritty Gene's crew is.

Jenn has been on a number of climbs and hikes with Gene over the years, but she's been worried about going out with him since his pacemaker started acting up while they were in the Enchantments last summer. A few months later, his pacemaker failed. His wife did CPR on their bedroom floor and he survived, but he lost some of his short-term memory. Sometimes the beginning of a conversation gets lost by the end, and has to be repeated. His wife cut him off from any climbing that involved a rope. Making the best of a bad situation, Jenn and I are going to borrow his rack. Jenn says she thinks he might even forget he'd lent it to us.

Gene still gets out on a lot of climbs that don't involve ropes. Right now, he's focused on finishing his e-guide book, *Guide to 100 Peaks at Mount Rainier National Park*. He only has a few peaks left to go.

Vivi and I drive over to The Mountaineers Program Center to meet up with Gene, but we can't find him. I think maybe he's forgotten about meeting me, and I'm about to start trying to track him down at his house when one of the other old guys who haunt the clubhouse says that Gene went on a day hike yesterday, one of the hundred peaks, and he hasn't come back. He's heard that Gene's SPOT—his personal locator beacon—has been activated, and thinks he'd been planning to hike with Gretchen, one of Gene's best friends, but he doesn't know anything more.

This leads me to immediate conjecture. Gretchen is a doctor, and she's pushing two decades in SMR, but there isn't much anybody could do if Gene's pacemaker quit again on the way up to some high point where no one ever goes, miles into Mount Rainier National Park where there is no cell phone service. It's not hard to picture Gretchen holding Gene's lifeless body in her arms as the sun set last evening, and then her pushing the button on his SPOT.

My phone is burning a hole in my back pocket. We were called out for a SPOT activation at Mount Rainier three hours ago. But I didn't go then, because I was going on vacation. Damn vacations.

Gretchen is pretty strong—she's climbed all kinds of stuff and goes on an expedition somewhere cool almost every year. When Gene dislocated his shoulder on a climb a few years back, Gretchen popped it back in and they kept going. She's good at taking extraordinary situations in stride. She and Russ once went on a search for a snowboarder who ended up in the Middle Fork Valley for three days. Eventually they tracked him down alive, but he did lose both his legs to frostbite. The snowboarder was so cold he'd started to lose it. He'd taken his liners out of his plastic boots and was wearing just the shells. He said he saw shadowy figures that looked vaguely Native American shuffling away from him in the snow, and he followed them. Right after he was found, a helicopter dropped a load of additional supplies. It ended up being so much stuff that the teams couldn't carry it all out, so a few days later Russell put together a little ski expedition to retrieve the gear.

The crew stopped for lunch once they reached the huge gear jumble, and Gretchen joked that the Native American spirits that apparently lived in this place might feel that they'd appropriated the gear that had been left. She suggested that everyone leave some sort of gift to make up for the gear they were going to pick up and take off with. So everybody left a bite of sandwich, or some candy or a carrot stick. Everybody except Jonas, who was hungry. But then, while skiing out, Jonas started having trouble breathing. Russ took his backpack, but after a mile Jonas was about to collapse, and Gretchen got to pull out her mad skill set. It could have been a curse, or it could have been in some way related to Jonas's history of spontaneously collapsed lungs.

Either way, I know Gretchen has good sense, and knows how to handle a crisis. Still, the idea of Gene being possibly dead is heavy, and I want Jenn and me to be there with the rest of the crew, to be supportive, even if the park is in the best position to help her.

I do know that Jenn will be devastated if Gene is dead. Jenn is already emotionally fragile because, during a dinner party earlier in the week, her good friend Mike had a massive stroke and collapsed at the table. Most of the people at the dinner party, which was in a rural area, had been nurses. So they carried him out to the car and drove to meet the ambulance, but he died anyway. Jenn came over later with Banjo, her large black-and-white fluffy dog, and a six pack of beer, and cried sitting at my back patio table after drinking half of one.

"It's so strange for climbers to die from something besides climbing," said Jenn. "It feels unnatural."

I said that I can't stand it when people say that someone died doing what they loved.

"But at least people can say something, what platitudes do you get when someone dies over a plate of spaghetti?" Jenn asked. "It's distressingly worse."

I call Jenn to tell her about Gene, and she leaves toddler story time at the library in tears. I tell her to get her stuff, that I'll drop off Vivi with my mom, pick her up, and we'll go down to the park and find Gene.

"But I'm not ready for that," Jenn says on the phone, and I can picture her seeking out a private place to talk, ending up standing in the library bathroom talking to me next to the courtesy sharps container, wearing purple Converse shoes and a hot-pink read-a-thon T-shirt.

"See you in half an hour," I tell her.

Gene left the Owyhigh Lakes Trailhead at 6:45 a.m. the day before to climb Double Peak. While I'm driving, Jenn calls his wife, who tells us that this was to be his ninety-fifth peak in the park. It was supposed to take two days, he was going to bivy somewhere on the route. I've never been to Double Peak. I suppose few people have. Jenn looks up the route description: it gains a little over 4,000 feet in eight miles. Gene would have had to kick steps in the snow for the second half. We start calling his main climbing partners, and figure out what gear he has with him, and we find out that he sent a message via his SPOT saying he got to the top at 5 p.m. last evening. Jenn calls Gretchen. We know there's no cell phone service, but we keep calling her anyway. Maybe she'll appreciate the messages later.

Then I get pulled over for speeding. I was speeding, but strangely enough it wasn't because I meant to. I've never actually gotten a speeding ticket before, and I've always thought somehow that if I ever got caught speeding, it would be because I was doing it on purpose. Furtively pushing just too far beyond that squishy line where I'm over the limit but still feel like the deputy won't bother with a traffic stop. Normally, I never speed. I drive like a grandma when I'm headed to the grocery store—I have a kid in the car, for goodness sake. It's just trying to weigh the gravity of the call I'm going to with knowing that I have to be careful. I've heard all the stories about aid crews plowing down pedestrians on their way to save someone with a sprained ankle. I will never become a cautionary tale.

I have to be doubly careful because I'm not a first responder. Fire trucks can speed legally, and fire fighters put union stickers on their cars and get professional courtesy from police officers even when they're not on duty. Police officers won't ticket each other. Mountain rescue doesn't have the same sort of relationship, but even if we did, I wouldn't want a sticker. If I identify myself with a sticker or even a patch on my jacket, then I have to be perfect. I can't call myself good at what I do if I'm doing something wrong; all I'd be doing is dragging the reputation of the group into the dirt with me. How do I know I can always be above reproach like a real professional? Fire fighters are the second-most respected profession in the US. I've read that they're second only to nurses, except for the year after the 9/11 attacks, when they were first. An image like that has to be carefully guarded, and always to be perfect in all things . . . it's a tall order.

But I'm not trying to speed. I feel sure that Gene is already dead. I just missed the city limits sign in Black Diamond, where the speed limit goes from 50 to 35. The only upside of being pulled over is that Jenn quits crying because we both feel the immediate need to look upstanding and presentable. I fold the ticket carefully and put it in the glove box next to my collection of park passes, the glow-in-the-dark Madonna, and a set of plastic utensils.

As soon as we get to the park, a helicopter locates Gene. They can see him down below them. He's waving.

Gretchen says later that she and a girlfriend had planned to meet up with Gene as he neared the top of Double Peak, but the brush was so bad that they'd turned around while Gene continued on alone.

Gene, when he tells the story later, says that the brush was terrible, so in trying to avoid large tracts of devil's club that he'd bushwhacked through on his way up, he'd veered off of his ascent route on the way down, ending up in a steep gully which wasn't indicated on the USGS topo. While crossing the gully in the dark, he slipped, caught his right crampon, and felt his right leg snap at the boot line. So, after thinking about that for a minute, he used his right knee and left leg, combined with the ample vegetation handholds, to drag himself about 150 feet back uphill and out of the gully to a nice bivy spot, where he sent another SPOT message that said, "I'm OK, bivy here tonight." This he decided to do because he didn't want to cause a night-time callout or wake up his primary or secondary SPOT contacts, choosing rather to wait until 7 a.m. the next day if he had to cause a bother.

I'm amazed by how often I think people are dead when in fact they're not. Its all conjecture, grasping at things half seen like apparitions in the Middle Fork. I have to keep reminding myself to believe that people are alive. Maybe if I thought Gene was alive, I would have gotten a speeding ticket for speeding on purpose. In the end, maybe I would have felt better about it that way.

Larry shuttles Gene's car around to the White River Ranger Station, where the park's contract helicopter eventually drops Gene off with us—Jenn won't let him leave until she's given him a hug—and then Larry drives him to the hospital.

Jenn and I are standing around talking to Pie and a couple other guys who've driven down with Everett Mountain Rescue as we're all getting ready to head home, when the Park asks us if we can look for another seventy-year-old guidebook author who is also missing after leaving the Owyhigh Lakes Trailhead yesterday. She was day hiking with a friend, but the friend wasn't comfortable in the snow so they agreed that she'd go on just for a bit to take some pictures, and then they'd meet back up at the car. But she didn't come back.

It's late afternoon when we start hiking up toward Owyhigh Lakes. The weather is changing, it's going to start raining soon. The snow is crusty with dirty black ridges. It's weathered all of the spring and will last at least another month in this place before any green shoots make it through. We can walk on top of it for the most part, but every once in a while we unexpectedly sink thigh-deep until our feet touch the sodden dirt underneath. The lakes are mostly unfrozen, with less snow around them and dead grass surrounding the edges. The ground looks solid, but stepping on it soaks our trail-runners and leaves water-filled footprints outlined in the bank.

It's very quiet. Then a helicopter comes in and drops off a dog team, and then it's quiet again. The incident commander from the park wants us to get back to the trailhead by dark. We're guests here, so we don't ask why. We search around the lakes, and then the IC asks us if we can take a drainage back to the trailhead, so we side-hill a long way, crossing tiny streams with steep snowbanks, working down the drainage and yelling the woman's name, but hearing nothing.

We turn around with enough time to get back before dark. It's always disorienting to go to a place that doesn't do much searching at night. Back home, almost everything we do happens after midnight. Searching at night in the woods has never made me uncomfortable.

Back in the parking lot, Jenn realizes that the stitching on her back pants pocket has unraveled, and her wallet fell out at some point between the trailhead, the lakes, the drainage, and the trailhead again. She has a sentimental attachment to the wallet, on top of not really wanting to replace the contents, so we go back to the White River Ranger Station at dusk to sign out from the search party. Then we drive back to the trailhead to hike up and retrace all our steps, looking for the wallet.

By the time we drive back to the Owyhigh Lakes Trailhead, it is fully dark and starting to rain. We spend a long night of drainage diving looking for the wallet, but, big surprise, we can't find it. We don't find the missing woman, either, although we do keep yelling her name, just in case. So, soaking wet, we return to the trailhead at midnight.

"Cold, wet, and scared . . . of identity theft," I say, putting the car in gear.

"You misunderstand the definition of vacation," says Jenn.

"Vacation is time off from work," I tell her. "Technically, my whole life is one long vacation. Welcome to vacationing with me."

Jenn digs through her pack and comes up with a chocolate bar in a baggie. She unwraps it and hands me half. I drop Jenn off at her house at 3 a.m. She wants to spend the day dealing with cancelling her credit cards, and trying to see what she can do about making up the work she missed. I can see that the Yosemite trip, already a big plan for a tight time frame, isn't coming together. When a trip starts to go sideways, it's best not to hang on too tight.

The guidebook author used to hike with my mother-in-law, so Russell goes down to the park to look for her an hour after I get home. That leaves nobody to watch Vivi while I go to Yosemite, clinching the trip's demise, but as I examine my feelings about it, Yosemite seems farther away than it ever used to be.

The search crews look so thoroughly and carefully that day that they even find Jenn's wallet, submerged in a creek. At first the searcher from Tacoma is excited to have found it, wondering if it could be a clue belonging to the missing woman or, failing that, if there is cash inside this dingy artifact from another time. But then, flipping out the driver's license, she realizes it was Jenn's, and she knows Jenn; the three of us went climbing in Squamish last Fourth of July—number two on my list of less than five truly relaxing vacations. She returns the wallet. And Jenn is happy.

Another searcher in another creek found the guidebook author, dead for a few days. I never found out why. I always find it jarring to learn I have been calling for someone who was already dead. Whether someone is alive or dead. It's such a strange thing not to know.

Vivian and Jenn and I find a short trip we can all do together in the time left—kayaking around Ross Lake in the North Cascades. I take the wooden double kayak Russell built for me a few years ago, and a single for Jenn. We put in, wading up to our knees in opaque blue glacial melt. Even with just my toes in this water, it's cold enough to make my teeth hurt. Vivi sits in the front hatch doing whatever she wants, waving her umbrella, washing her rock collection, or flopping mostly out of the hatch, balanced on the hot deck in the hot sunshine while I paddle us around. Jenn does circles around us, a little spot of yellow in a blue lake.

Then I come back and pick my dates for traffic school. I can't have even a single traffic infraction on my record and expect to get hired.

LITTLE SI

I DIDN'T GO BACK TO paramedic school. I think I'd be a good paramedic, but getting a job as one is inexorably linked to being a fire fighter, and I'm wary of trying that again, afraid that despite my best efforts I won't be good enough, that I'll have wasted more of everybody's time and my family's support. The day before school started, I jumped ship. "It takes sticking to something to be successful at it," says Russ, and I know he's right.

I always wanted to be the girl who could prove that women could do anything, but now that I've tried and failed my way into middle age, I think failing is a disservice to the cause of womanhood, because I'm reinforcing the negative stereotype that women wash out, screwing the other ladies who come after me, and I have to live both with my failure and knowing I helped make other women's lives harder too.

Or, possibly, my conundrum isn't about being a woman at all. I listened to a podcast once about how, as women, we tend to use gender as an excuse when bad things happen to us, when the reality is that sometimes people just have trouble admitting they aren't smart enough to do the job, or skilled enough to do the job, or they just didn't try hard enough.

I tend to overthink things. Occam's razor: The simplest explanation is usually right. I'm probably just not strong enough. I decide to go after some other job, a job where the requirements are tangible and objective.

On the same day I drop out of paramedic school, I register for a full load of nursing prerequisites, begin classes, and Vivian starts first grade. I've taken a lot of math and most of the basic natural-world classes when I went to college the first time, but, irritatingly, they're only good for so many years, so I have to take them all again. I also start filling out applications to be a hospice volunteer. Getting into a nursing program requires a resume with a large amount of volunteer work specifically working with nurses. And also, I think being a hospice nurse is something I could do in the end.

So I'm filling out this hospice volunteer application, sitting at the kitchen table in the middle of the night, long after Russ and Vivi have gone to bed. "Have you ever been with someone when they died?" I check the electronic YES bubble. "What are your thoughts on death?" There is a single fill-in-the-blank line, space for maybe fifteen words. I can't speak to how many applications I've filled out over the past six years, but this question is a new one. I stare at the screen while the cursor flashes. And flashes.

Ten months later, in June, after organic chemistry, biology, math and three dozen rescues, and after talking my way out of retaking English 101, two high school boys found bones on Mount Si. The bones were just below the Haystack, a meander downhill from the trail. I'm sure the boys wondered if they were human or not, because they couldn't find a skull. Maybe if hunting runs in your family it's not so hard to tell if a bone belongs to a person or an animal, but there's that nagging worry that you will look silly if you call 911 and it turns out to be the remains of a deer. But then they found the white, old-school sneakers with socks—and feet—still in them, and I'm pretty sure that clinched it.

Garth and I hiked the boys back up the trail so they could show us where they'd seen the body. Garth's daughter's cross-country team was poised to win the state championship, and Garth is dedicated to running with her no matter how much it hurts him. I wasn't sure how much longer he could do it, since she just gets faster every year, but the practice paid off—in the parking lot one of the boys expressed his feelings about having to hike back up with us old folks, and so we smoked them.

The King County Sheriff's Office was taking the opportunity to do helicopter training for their deputies. We were supposed to hike up and find the human remains, and then the deputies would winch out of the helicopter to do the investigation, and then we'd pick up all the bones we could find.

A giant mechanical bird with a winch, heat sensors, night-vision goggles, and a couple of deputies can do my job better than I can. It's evolution. Helicopters are expensive, noisy, and impersonal, and they crash sometimes; you could get in with a sprained ankle, and end up as a pile of crushed char. But most of the time, they work fine.

If I'm critically injured somewhere way the heck out there and really want to get to Harborview in less than an hour and the weather's good, please send the helicopter, but if I'm dead, going to be dead soon no matter what, or pretty likely to pull through, I'd rather have my crew. Human connection, caring, isn't our stated goal as SAR volunteers. Maybe I'm the only one who thinks it matters. But let my crew come get me.

The body on Little Si had been there a long time, so long that a tree had grown through the ribs. Roots spread through the tattered clothes held together with string and underwear elastic. Duff covered the pelvic bones, the little green backpack and avalanche gear from the '90s.

The only tool we'd brought was a mini-hatchet that looked like a Klingon prop from *Star Trek*—Pete the deputy is really good at scrounging up military surplus stuff—and we ended up using it as a rake to get everything human out of the stump. We didn't find any identification in the backpack. We couldn't find the skull, either, but sometimes animals drag body parts a long way, and heads, being round, tend to roll downhill. I shuffled around looking for it in holes and under ferns. Peering over the top of another old stump nearby, I found a robin's nest, soft with feathers and woven with bits of string and underwear elastic, holding three tiny, brilliant blue eggs.

For twenty years this person lay here, just a few feet from the busiest hiking trail in Washington State. I've walked this trail hundreds of times, and it's odd not to have known. It's just a thing that happens, I suppose. There must be dead people everywhere.

So that was in mid-June. Between then and mid-September there were thirty-seven more rescues, including one for a thrown rider and stranded horse that required two days, a variety of organizations, technical lowers, trail building, and a horse-sized plastic sled. There was a girl who fell over a dry waterfall, broke her back, and tore her aorta, but lived. It was 100 degrees that day. I emptied my little EMT kit and then sat with her for an hour, waiting for the helicopter and acting as a human sunshade. Oyvind, now part of the helicopter team for Snohomish County, eventually winched down and grabbed her— King County's helicopter was busy at Seafair. I yelled a short report at him, and he shouted back, "Hope Russ and Vivi are doing well!"

There was dehydration and benightedness and a mission for a man with an injured toe. He'd hurt it diving into a lake. Nothing hurts like toe pain. Garth helped him limp back to the parking lot.

In September, a hiker and his dog went past a "Trail Closed" sign at Twin Falls. The trail was closed because it was washed out. The dog slipped and got stuck partway down the washout. The man tried to get the dog, and fell to his death in the river. The dog was fine.

A week later a man hanged himself on a golf course. The initial call said, "Man lost in golf course," and we were wondering how that was possible, but we figured it out. He didn't get lost. He was in the woods on the golf course property. One of the search-dog handlers found him. I think sometimes people are drawn into the woods when they feel it's their time. Maybe it's just that the woods are a sacred space, unmarred, mysterious, and quiet. All people through all the ages of the world have returned to nature, so it doesn't seem so strange to me that people would do it now.

Two days later, we went to look for human remains in the ski area at Snoqualmie Pass. Someone had found a little camp with personal belongings in it. Ed put the information about the camp together with a report of a car that had been towed from the parking area months before, and eventually sold at auction. Then he traced it back to a missing persons report, and from there to an owner who presumably was in these woods. They called us out to rappel down a series of cliffs because they thought he might have jumped, but we found a few bags worth of his bones within minutes of starting to look around the campsite.

Less than a week later, we got called out to look for a lost hiker with dementia on Tiger Mountain. Lost and demented. The call came during Seattle Mountain Rescue's monthly board meeting, a presentation on how to do presentations to school groups, and I was remembering the production that Jenn, Drew, and I had done for a class of fifth graders a few weeks before. We created mass chaos. We arrived with enough gear that our knees were about to buckle, and we yelled out that we needed volunteer rescuers for a half dozen "climbers" who fell off a cliff.

"You guys," Jenn yelled, pointing out a half dozen kids, "are all really hurt because you weren't wearing helmets."

She was in charge of staging the scene.

"Now I want you to scream and roll around on the floor when the rescuers get here." There was a lot of giggling, and many strange death poses.

Drew directed the rescue: "Quick! Who wants to save the lives of your friends? Look! That one's got blood spurting out of his leg!"

Fifth graders love to volunteer, but more than that, they are good at this job they've never done before. They're strong, they follow directions, they learn quickly, and they aren't hampered by the knowledge of what happened last time. And they save everybody. Nobody ever dies. They can handle a mass casualty incident, start to finish, before the lunch bell. If only we were as good as they are.

I didn't go on the search for the man with dementia on Tiger Mountain. I should have gone, maybe, but people are not usually very hard to find when they get lost in an area with cell phone service. They might not know where they are, but the sheriff's office can get GPS coordinates from anyone's cell phone in a couple of minutes, whether they call 911 or not. Then all you have to do is walk up to the coordinates, and there's the lost hiker.

Years ago, before cell phones, it took a lot of people to find someone, and it still does in the Middle Fork because there's no cell phone service in that valley. But in the past few years, since carrying a cell phone has become ubiquitous, if there's phone service it only takes one person and four or five hours to find someone in the middle of the night.

The night of the mission for the man with dementia on Tiger Mountain, I was coming up on a microbiology exam. Getting into nursing school is painfully competitive. I know it's just an undergrad thing at a junior college, a place for high school dropouts, English language learners, other stay-at-home moms trying to become dental hygienists. It's funny, though, because I took these classes the first time at a real university, and the coursework and the difficulty of the exams is actually the same. But now I have to get perfect grades. It takes so much time.

Still, it's not actual work. Even Ed the SAR Deputy, when he calls me at home to have me plan large rescues, tells me that it's time to put down the remote.

"Hey, Mommy," he says, "turn off *Jerry Springer* and put your bon bons back in the freezer."

"Okay," I tell him, even though I don't know what a bon bon looks like.

I needed to buckle down and study, so I didn't go search for the man with dementia. But he was found okay after an hour or so, his coordinates retrieved, and then he was reunited with his wife.

Two weeks later, I'm driving home from my night class when we get called out for a disoriented hiker on Little Si, just outside North Bend city limits. I'm still a long ways from home, still in Seattle, when SMR's In Town Operations Leader calls and tells me I have to go. Technically, I don't have to go, but whoever's currently on ITOL duty tends to call me when they haven't gotten anyone with enough experience to commit to being in charge of the SMR crew. They call me because I tend to say yes. This time I say I'll do it because Little Si is, well, a little foothill next to Big Si, which is just a slightly bigger foothill, and I figure that it won't take too long, and I can still get some studying in afterwards. I have to guard these quiet hours after Russ and Vivi go to bed pretty carefully.

I have to stop by my house to pick up my gear because I'm afraid to keep it in my car at school. It's basically everything of financial value that I own. I'm too cheap to pay for parking on campus—I've been parking behind the Sears and walking the half mile, which I don't mind, except that there's always broken glass on the ground behind Sears.

When I get home, Russell and Vivian are asleep. I think about fire fighters leaving for a call in ninety seconds, already stationed strategically near the emergency. I think about how far it is from Seattle to North Bend with a stop in Carnation, how I live in Carnation because I can't afford to live in North Bend. I think about how many minutes this stop takes me. It's too many. I'm going to be too late. I float like a ghost blown by a gale through my house, a silent black whirr. I change my clothes and get out the front door with all my gear in less than ninety seconds. I do it in total darkness and quietly enough not to wake anyone up. And the ninety seconds includes getting my school clothes into the dirty clothes hamper, because leaving them on the floor drives Russell crazy. I also manage to grab a bag of organic sweet potato tortilla chips to eat for dinner.

Maybe after a certain point it doesn't matter when I get there. The old SAR saying is that by the time you get there, the person who called for help is either going to be fine, or they're already dead. The problem is that I don't believe this is the case with the advent of GPS-enabled cell phones. Now we get there sometimes before people bleed out, if we're fast enough. And no matter what their condition, the person or their family always wants help as soon as possible.

I make a plan as I drive, because I'll need it by the time I get there, because I'll be behind already, but the plan has to be maximally adaptable to account for anything on earth that could have happened already. I'm stuffing chips into my mouth because I'm hungry, and I'm shifting gears, and I have another microbiology exam the next day, and I want to know why these things line up the way they do. I don't even have a job. Why do I feel like I can't keep up? I should trust that the rest of my crew will be fine, and go home and study. They almost always are—I pause and think about that. I'm an egomaniac. But maybe I just want to see them. Just want to feel good about doing something more meaningful today than studying mold all alone in the lab. Just want to be a part of something awesome. It's about me wanting to make some kind of difference in the world, to help one more person and feel good about it even though I know it means I'm not looking out for my own best interests. My own keep. My own child. This is me risking a lifetime of serial, overreaching failures. I slap myself in the face. Little pieces of tortilla chip land everywhere. No wonder my husband thinks I'm a slob.

I walk over to Eric, the ESAR Operations Leader, standing with a clipboard in the Little Si parking lot surrounded by 4x4s with their lights flashing. He says the man fell and hurt his arm, but doesn't know exactly where he is. The man's pretty confused, but we have his coordinates. No helicopter tonight—the trees are too thick.

I'm Team 7 or so with Jarek, a quiet engineer and accomplished Polish sport climber. It's been a couple of hours since the mission started. When Jarek and I are halfway up the trail, Team 1 finds the man unconscious, having trouble breathing, a long way from the trail. Not an arm injury. Team 1 calls for paramedics. Tonight their paramedic comes with a fire fighter entourage.

Jarek and I turn around and start jogging back toward the parking lot to meet up with the fire department, because Eric has asked if we can help them carry their stuff in. About the time we meet up with the fire department, Team 1 calls over the radio and says the man has quit breathing. They can't find a pulse, and they're starting CPR.

The crew that shows up on the trail with the fire medics is the career crew I used to be assigned to when I was a volunteer at East-side Fire and Rescue. I run into this fire crew every time I go to the grocery store. I've started shopping in another town. Here they are again. They won't let us carry any of their stuff. That would look like they couldn't carry it as fast as we could. That isn't the case because they're professionals and we're amateurs, so of course they can carry whatever needs to be carried faster, farther, and more professionally.

I know they can carry their own stuff, and I also know that speed doesn't matter too much any more. The man is having a traumatic arrest, too far from an operating room. None of us can fix it.

But the biggest issue for me is that EMTs can't declare anyone dead, only a paramedic or a doctor can, and so until the paramedics arrive, somewhere in the dark in the bushes, under a thick canopy of black trees, Team 1 is stuck doing endless CPR. They're asking over the radio for a pocket mask, so they're doing endless

CPR with—hopefully they have some sort of barrier device, and not doing mouth to mouth. They're not from SMR. They're good guys who are used to helping us carry people out, not ending up in situations like this. And I'm pretty sure they went in thinking that, if anything, they were going to sling and swath an arm. If I feel urgency, it's mostly wishing them mercy, not because I'm deluded that I can help save someone's life.

The man is maybe a quarter mile off the trail in a place with a lot of bushes and little rock bands. Getting there requires some steep side-hilling. Some of the ESAR guys didn't feel comfortable on the terrain and so they're waiting for us back near the trail. I have them give their helmets to the fire crew, and while the fire crew is trying to negotiate the slope, I go on ahead to the man. He is pretty large. He's on his back, lying half on a huge nurse log, green with moss; the bark has peeled back dark orange where Team 1 has been kneeling against it. I recognize Chris and Matt, ESAR guys; their headlights bounce in the dark as they do CPR.

"Can you help us?" Matt asks. I think about it for a second and say no. The Fire Department will be here in a minute and they'll feel obligated to take over doing CPR for another few minutes before declaring the man dead. I know the paramedic is going to want to get a tube out of it—he has to intubate so many people in a year to maintain his certification, so he'll use this opportunity to practice. When they're done, he'll pull out his tube and say the man's dead. Then the Fire Crew will pack it up and leave to get back in service, on to the next call, or, because the night is pretty slow, go back to the station, take showers, and go to bed. Either way, they'll be ready in ninety seconds for the next emergency. It's comforting to know someone will be there in a timely manner.

I'm going to stay here, with the man. This is my only emergency until my microbiology exam. And what kind of an emergency is that, anyway? I can't die from a bad grade. I can risk something to be here. I would want someone to stay with me.

I have a focus problem; somehow it's myopic and too wide of a lens at the same time. I'm good at the work because I'm focused in the moment, always there when someone needs me, paying attention, and at the same time I'm thinking that this moment is one of the most important ones in someone's entire life: the day your life flashes before your eyes, or the day you die. How all the millions of tiny nagging concerns, life's little failures, the daily grind—how it all falls away, and you get a glimpse of what life really means, the human connection that binds us together, standing shoulder to shoulder with the people you care about, watching the cosmic dance under a star-choked sky. But I have to remember that the middle stuff—the daily grind—it needs to matter more to me. Getting into nursing school requires ambition, fire-service jobs require a pound of flesh, living requires making money, and if I don't spend enough time looking out for my own best interests, nobody else will, either. And with that, I know what it is that I need to do.

Now I'm volunteering with hospice on Wednesdays, and it's hard not to stay in my power curve. One of the major tenets is that when you're there, you need to be really present. You leave your own drama and your own story at the door, and really listen. I like hospice. I want to be able to do this now, on Little Si.

I put my hand on Matt's shoulder. His shirt is soaked with sweat. The fire department is almost here. "Good work, Matt," I say. Matt is still busy. I lean over the man. "I'm sorry," I tell him. "Sometimes you can do everything right, and it still doesn't work out. We did our best and you did your best and we ended up here, but now we're here with you and we'll stay as long as you need us."

I'm going to send Matt back down the trail to take the fire department folks to the parking lot. Then Chris, the guys who aren't comfortable on the terrain, and any last people who might be coming are going to work together to carry this man back home.

The time still matters. I can't help Matt push more blood out of this man's circulatory system. I need to make some phone calls and see about getting more people, and rigging gear, a litter, and a body bag here now. Matt is touching the man. Maybe the important part at this stage is just to know that he was touched by someone.

At hospice, after someone dies and the family leaves, the nurse puts a candle in the room's window. Here we stand in the dark, surrounding him. Each of us with a light. A lumen is a unit of luminous flux, equal to the amount of light emitted per second in a unit solid angle of one steradian from a uniform source of one candela. Each of our headlamps has a hundred lumens. As a group we twinkle, interwoven, roving light.

It's midnight.

"We know him," says Chris, bent over and still doing chest compressions. "We found him two weeks ago on Tiger Mountain. He got lost, and we took him back to his wife."

Was it one of those times when someone found their way into the woods because they knew it was time? How would I know? Maybe I hope it's true because this idea helps me, but I know equally well not to tell it to the widow. It's a platitude, and no better than, "He's in a better place," which would be a lie since by the time I'd be in a position to tell her that, he'd be with the medical examiner. Another one I hate is, "Everything happens for a reason." I don't believe in a grand plan, or why, if there were a grand plan, this kind of thing would be part of it. The worst platitude, usually said with a smile and a hand squeeze is, "Maybe this was necessary for growth." Sometimes people do grow as they deal with a tragedy. But sometimes they're ruined. Diminished forever, recognizing that some part of themselves, no longer reflected, has left. Grief is exhausting, and being tasked with using loss to grow stronger—or else feel you betrayed the dead and their sacrifice for your benefit, which you've squandered—is even more so.

After the fire crew leaves, I take pictures for the medical examiner. Following dirt scuffs, we find the man's phone a ways above him. He must have fallen multiple times. We get the rigging gear, the ropes, and the litter. There wasn't a body bag available, or maybe nobody was left to carry it. Everyone needs to get to work in the morning. My daughter is sleeping in her bed. Russell leaves for work at five o'clock no matter what. I have to make sure we're back to the trailhead by 4:30 in order to get home on time.

We stretch the ropes out between trees, sinking to our shins in the loose dirt. It's steep enough that when I stand up, my uphill shoulder is in the ferns. We do not have enough people, just five for the rigging and carry combined. Paul is space-hauling off a tree from above, shiny black ponytail sticking out from under his helmet, and I have three people pulling forward with maximal exertion, with the man in the litter tied to what is essentially a series of zip lines. The trees are too short and we can't get high enough to take more than a little of his weight. We move a few inches at a time across the slope.

I'm not going to leave. I said I wouldn't. I can feel the late night becoming early morning. I should probably say "no" more in the beginning, but once I'm committed to something, I'll see it through. My crew makes groaning noises each time they lurch forward with the body. There's not much power left. The litter sags down during the lifts and I'm afraid someone will hurt their back. This guy weighs more than Paul and Jarek put together. I eyeball the small blue tarp I wrapped around the man's head and torso, and look down toward his boots, judging size. Yes. He is large.

I can see a light coming toward me, and then Patrick shows up. Hours ago, I asked Steve to call everyone on the roster that he thought might be willing to come. It's always an awkward thing, waking possible responders up in the middle of the night because not enough people have answered the text messages, especially if you do it all the time. Some of the conversations can get prickly. "You need me? How badly do you need me? What exactly will happen if I don't come? Where is this? So, this thing is not actually in the mountains then. So, what you're saying is that nobody is really going to die because he's already dead, so. . . ."

One side of Patrick's face is swollen. "Root canal," he says, "but hey, you needed help?" "Thanks," I say. "Really, thanks."

Patrick is strong, still in his twenties for another two months, muscular without trying. He told me once that he never really has to try very hard at anything, he's the kind of guy that didn't study in school because he knew more than the professors. And tonight he's got this, bringing agile joyful power. Bringing success. I get home at 4:50.

I crawl into bed, but can't sleep. Russell's clock radio goes off a few minutes later. He likes classic rock, Aerosmith and Tom Petty. This morning it's *The Dark Side of the Moon*. "Run. Rabbit, Run," says Roger Waters. Russ hits the top of the black cube, says nothing to me. Once he's gone I take his warm spot, and I still can't sleep.

Eleven days later I'm out again. I'm holding the distal end of a small tree branch so Pete the deputy can try chopping it off flush with the trunk. When someone hangs themselves, it's important for the investigation to get the noose with the knot intact. But after Pete hacks at the slender branch for a long time with his ridiculous Klingon mini-axe, the branch finally splits length-wise and the white extension cord slides off.

We bag the extension cord along with the entire branch. Only green bones are left under the branch, plus clothes and a backpack. We stuff the bones we can find into red biohazard bags.

A hunter found the body a few days ago. He called 911 to report it, standing in the woods in the rain, but apparently he'd been transferred, and while waiting to talk to the right detective, he'd heard an elk bugle—so he hung up to continue the hunt before the sheriff's office could get his GPS coordinates. He was a conscientious guy, though. He called again, post-hunt, and took a deputy back up to show him the spot. But this time he brought his son, it was pouring buckets of rain, and getting dark, and the deputy ended up piggy-backing the kid out without doing a full investigation.

But at least the deputy got the dead person's backpack. I watched Ed go through it. There was no ID, but a small Tupperware container full of quarters, along with a lot of spiders and an empty wine bottle. Eventually Ed figured out who the man was by using the dates on the quarters to help pinpoint when he went missing. Ed is a genius at this.

We find his skull by a stump, and carry it out in a red biohazard bag along with femurs, a scapula, and a clavicle I found in a fern. It is only raining harder today. A stream of water drips off my nose. The trail is a muddy, funneling torrent as we hike back out.

Two weeks later, there's another suicide: a truck, a camp, and bones lying next to a pocket pussy, remarkably well preserved. Ed uses his short, mostly useless Klingon-axe to break a window of the man's truck. It takes a number of tries, but Ed says that it's because he doesn't want to accidentally hit the window too hard and put his hand through the glass, not because the tool doesn't work. Eventually the window breaks, and he retrieves the thirty-page suicide note describing boredom with life, along with two empty bags of potato chips, and half the man's lower jaw. Ed thinks tweakers have probably been here and placed the jaw in the cab some time ago.

Another two weeks pass, and there's a recovery for a man who hanged himself. His head is still attached but won't be for much longer. Steve found him. Steve's a religious guy. He told me once that he couldn't understand why anybody would kill themselves. It's strange that he finds so many people who have.

Then I run into Ed while we're looking for a backcounty skier who did not kill himself; he just disappeared while skiing near Kendall Stump after a storm dumped two and a half feet of new snow at Snoqualmie Pass—the final storm in a series of storms. It's the second day of the search. The first day I was out skiing, searching with Nick and Taylor.

A number of folks in SMR had known the skier. Nick knew him. Nick joined SMR after his wife died in a base jumping incident. In a strange small-world coincidence, he and his current roommates were friends with the skydivers I found the day I discovered I was pregnant with Vivian. Nick has since gone back to base jumping, but he goes out on a lot of rescues with us, too.

We stopped on a little rise, and I fell over for no reason. I put my hand out, but there was nothing to land on and I ended up upside down with my skis inverted on the surface of the snow—not even in a tree well. A person can't breathe through snow; unable to move, or dig themselves out, they asphyxiate and die. I wasn't scared, which is a crazy thing when you can't breathe, but I knew Nick and Taylor would figure it out eventually.

Years ago, when I was a climbing bum living out of my car, I used to worry that if I was soloing and fell, nobody would even notice I was missing for a month. It takes Taylor maybe a minute to get out of his splitboard bindings, fight his way over to me, and shovel me out. He looks scared and Nick is yelling back, asking if I'm okay from his position knee-deep in the middle of the next creek we have to cross. All I can think, with snow stuck in my ears and up my nose, is how much respect I have for my friends, how I can't live without them.

The second day, sitting in base with Ed, he says that the latest news from KCSO is that Pete has gotten 200 more pounds of the short Klingon axes from the military, and a yellow snowcat. Ed shows me a picture of the snowcat on his phone, the camera flash glinting off the cab windows.

"What's it for?" I ask Ed.

"For doing SAR," says Ed. It looks new.

"Gosh," I say, "that's nice, I guess."

"The deputies are going to learn how to drive it," says Ed. "I also got this khaki shirt" he adds, holding out his arm so I can feel the fabric of the sleeve and show approval. This could be the first vaguely civilian shirt he's owned in thirty years. "It's a nice shirt, Ed," I tell him, but I'm worried that this could be an indication that he could get a civilian life together and retire.

We borrow the expansive conference room in the new Snoqualmie Pass Fire Station to use as our base because so many backcountry skiers from different SAR groups come to look that we need a place to organize them. I tell Ed I'm worried about someone from my crew drowning in the bottomless snow—snow immersion syndrome—because obviously this is on my mind. They're great skiers, but any-body can fall over, especially while searching terrain they wouldn't normally choose to ski. Ed says if I'm scared to go back out, he'll find another team leader. Ed promised the girlfriend we would get the skier. Maybe something in me has changed, because when he tells me I should spend the day sitting with the girlfriend, I say okay.

So Ed and I spend the rest of the morning and through the after-noon sitting on gray plastic chairs with the missing skier's girlfriend, drawn off-kilter together in the middle of the cavernous room, wait-ing for news. The teams drag back in at dusk. After this, Nick orga-nizes search after search, day after day, but we can't find the skier. Even after KCSO calls the official search off, the skier's girlfriend keeps going out every weekend to look for him, and I know some of the SMR guys go with her.

His girlfriend finds him after six months, in June, when the snow-pack finally melts out. That day we've flown a rigging instructor in from Colorado, but couldn't find a space to have the training, so we are in the middle of a seminar in Larry's backyard when Ed calls.

"I have to go," says Nick, but he's driven SMR-2 to the training and the truck has to stay.

"Think you can ride my motorcycle with your backpack on?" asks Larry. "I'm not sure how fast it goes, but I think you need to take it."

Nick gets on Larry's motorcycle and goes to do the recovery. Tay-lor joins him. Ed's able to keep his promise. The rest of us stay at the training. We paid for this instructor with money donated by the families of other people who died, and the rigging I'm learning—I'm about to need it.

These are all just things that happened, without a commonality in time, or place, or reason, or any other part. No one got saved except for me. After a certain point, nobody really expected us to save anyone. No point in using a first responder for someone who has been dead for two decades—this is a job that volunteers do. These people ended up where they did, and we saw what happened, we know the end of the story, read the note about being alone, or brought them back to the people who loved them because, well, I suppose it's just because we were the ones who showed up.

And then I showed up for my next volunteer shift at hospice, dropped my coat off in the tiny break room situated next to a gender-neutral bathroom. On one side there's a lamp with a twenty-watt bulb and the coat rack; on the other, a computer to sign in, a chair, and pictures of the visiting therapy dogs with their names written underneath in cursive.

The break room's heavy door swings shut with a click. There's a Maya Angelou quote taped to the wall. It says,

> *The thing to do, it seems to me, is to prepare yourself so that you can be a rainbow in somebody else's cloud. Somebody who may not look like you. May not call God the same name you call God—if they call God at all. I may not dance your dances or speak your language. But be a blessing to somebody. That's what I think.*

"Maya," I say, because I'm okay with talking to dead people, whether they're there or not, "I have to go work on a more tangible skill set for a while." I lean into the paper, until my nose almost touches it, and I whisper, "But I'll be back."

GRANITE: WEST RIDGE

EVERY NEW YEAR'S EVE, ABOUT forty members of Russ's mom's family get together for Chinese food. Social hour starts at five, dinner at six. It had been three years since we'd come, and Russ' mom had hinted that we should really consider upping our level of familial responsibility. So we were coming, but Russ got out of work late, so we weren't going to make it until almost six.

At 5:24 we got a text for a missing sixty-five-year-old snowshoer last seen on top of Granite. We pulled over in an Albertson's parking lot halfway between Carnation and the Chinese restaurant, and stared out the windshield with the car running, trying to decide where to go, and what the consequences would be if we didn't show up at the Eastern Pearl.

Jenn sent me a text. Paul had just picked her up from the airport after twenty-four hours of sleeplessness and delays on her way home from visiting her folks for Christmas. I'd been feeding Banjo all week. She wanted to know what my spidey sense said about this search. The snowshoer had been last seen at 4:30 on top of Granite—only about an hour ago. Most of the time, people don't report someone missing when they're only an hour late. She didn't want to drive all the way up the pass, only to turn around and drive all the way home again when what she really wanted to get home to her puppy and go to bed.

I texted Jenn back that, because he was an older guy, maybe he just walked slower than the rest of his party, and he'd be at the trailhead in an hour. Either that, or he could have broken an ankle somewhere high on the mountain, where there was still tons of snow blowing around in the dark from last week's storm, and if she didn't go then he would probably freeze to death before anybody else could get there. I looked up the forecast and it was predicted to be 11 degrees by midnight, not including windchill.

The thing about holidays is that it can be difficult to find people who are available to go search. The previous spring there had been a storm at Mount Rainier with 90-mile-per-hour winds, and Jenn was late coming back from Camp Muir. She'd missed the first day of her new job and hadn't come home to feed Banjo. Paul, who was also Jenn's emergency contact, called me to ask whether she'd been gone long enough to warrant calling the park to start looking for her. He was worried, because it was Super Bowl Sunday, that he wasn't going to be able to rally a sober contingent. But Russ doesn't like football, and I don't drink on the weekends. We picked up Taylor, who would have watched the game but agreed with us that Jenn doesn't weigh enough to hold a tent down in 90-mile-per-hour winds. We drove down together, thinking she was dead. But she wasn't. She walked out once the storm eased, and we met her in the parking lot at Paradise.

But this was New Year's Eve, which is even tougher than Super Bowl Sunday. It involves parties that people don't want to miss, and drinking, and spending time with family. Kissing your significant other at midnight. Ringing in a new year with cheer and a silly hat. SMR's ITOL texted that nobody had called in yet to say they were coming.

"We can stay at the Eastern Pearl for an hour," said Russ. "We promised my mom."

It boggles my mind that someone could literally freeze to death alone on an exposed, windswept ridge because I stopped for General

Tso's chicken. How possible that is. How hubristic that I think so, yet how possible it is.

Someone could die because I went to my chemistry midterm, or because I went to visit my grandma in Portland for her birthday, or because I spent an hour at the kids' table at the Eastern Pearl with the ten-and-under set drinking Shirley Temples, wondering what each deep fried dish was, since they all looked identical, and trying to get some plain white rice for Vivian so she'd eat something. But we did it. Our families put up with so much for us, and we'd promised to be there.

After fifty-nine minutes we went over to Debbie's table to say goodbye and make sure that Vivian could still spend the night at their house.

"Sure, there's a rescue. You just don't want to have to eat any more greasy Yushan chicken. Let's see your phone," said Russ's dad.

I held out my phone with a smile like a grimace.

"Happy New Year," I said to everyone. We apologized, and we left.

Before we got to the trailhead, Caley called and told us it was someone we knew. We tried calling Doug McCall to tell him that his cousin and main climbing partner was overdue. We'd run into McCall's cousin, whose name was also Doug, a few times in the mountains, and we'd climbed together in Squamish for a few days. McCall had told us enough stories that we knew Doug wasn't one of the old guys who takes his time. But McCall was still vacationing in Italy with his family. Russ called three times before he picked up.

I don't normally go out on rescues alone with Russ anymore. Sure, he's my husband, so we're alone together a lot, but on climbing trips and rescues we always split up or find a third party. Sometimes we tell people it's because, since we have a kid, if something bad happens, the bad thing'll only get one of us—but that isn't it, really. It's just that I think we hold each other to an unreasonable standard, and being a perfect partner in life is hard enough. Climbing is a whole 'nother thing.

But this time it made sense for us to go together because together we get a lot done, even if it makes us unhappy. The logistics were already tight. We were already late, so we didn't stop to do a lot of the things we'd normally do for a search, like make a thermos of hot tea, but at a certain point you just have to go.

The plan was to go up the ridge that Doug most likely took and, if we didn't find him on the way up, break into the Granite Mountain lookout at the top to spend the night. Russ used to volunteer for the Forest Service, opening and closing the lookout for the season. We knew it was closed up now, but Russ was pretty sure the secret key was still there, and he could find it.

While we were packing our gear in the back of Russell's truck, our feet sliding on inches of black ice in the parking lot, Ed minced over and offered us his "universal key," a nice pair of long-handled bolt cutters. I would have taken them, but I can never quite keep up with Russ even when I'm carrying nothing, and Russ didn't want to carry them because he knew he could find the key. He's confident like that. Like the last time we did something recreational alone together, five or six years ago when we went to climb the West Ridge of Stuart. He didn't want me to bring the topo I'd photocopied because he had the route memorized. "Okay," I said, and then we spent the night sharing a sixty-gallon industrial trash bag, which constituted all of our emergency bivy gear, listening to the mice nibble the grips off our trekking poles until dawn when we hiked out, and I recommitted to always climbing with a third party. This time, Russ told me he was a veritable key dowser. That whole Stuart thing was an isolated incident. He had the whole area memorized. There was no way we weren't going to get the key. "Okay," I said, because he does not usually lose track of things.

We packed snowshoes and crampons. Granite is a good ski, but you can't skin up it very easily, it's almost always a boot and carry— and it was dark and windy, and we were looking for Doug, who was also on snowshoes. I don't have the control to sled someone out on skis through this kind of terrain, anyway. If we found Doug, and he was injured, then the best I could do would be to tie lengths of webbing to the sides of the litter and have folks walk it down through the trees, doing lowers for the steeper spots. But we weren't going to carry a litter up right now, either; if we found Doug, someone else could bring it up. More folks had finally arrived. Caley was going to stay in base and plan where to send the rest of the teams, and get a gear cache started somewhere centrally located, maybe where the summer trail and the winter trails meet, in case we did need more equipment quickly. But we all agreed that it would be better if Russ and I just started up to the top, and the rest could get figured out while we worked our way up there.

A few SMR and volunteer ski patrol folks were already ahead of us going up the winter trail, which is a knee-deep posthole of improbably large steps cut steeply up to the western shoulder through the woods. Russ has an uncanny knowledge of almost every rise and hollow for fifty miles in every direction. He rarely gets confused but I don't like blindly following anybody. The trouble is that even if I get out my GPS, he always stays far enough ahead that he's a little out of earshot so I either have to follow, or split the team if I don't like where he's headed. It's irritating.

After an hour, we met up with the first group who'd left the trailhead ahead of us. I thought briefly that we could stay together, but Russ only has one speed, and we did need to go as fast as possible, and five minutes later their headlamps were out of sight behind us. We kept yelling for Doug and looking for any lights ahead of us, but I found it hard to differentiate a separate light source from the blowing snow whipping in front of the LED bulbs strapped to my forehead. It was just flashes of searing white, then black, then white again. Plus I still hadn't fixed the loose wire in my headlamp, and it turned itself off every few minutes. Forced to stop and fix the light, I looked up to see the strangest blood-orange slit of a moon just above the slope's rise. I thought it was an improbable bonfire; then I thought it was a supernatural thing. And then I saw it was the moon, and it was clear above the blowing snow.

People always overestimate wind speeds, so I try to aim low. It might have been gusting to thirty in the trees. Higher on the ridge, most of the snow had been blown away, and we climbed up steps of frozen heather encased in ice. I should have stopped lower down to put my heavier gloves on, but there was no stopping now, except to brace for a few seconds against the larger gusts. The wind was largely at my back, which was good because even with goggles protecting my eyes, the snow blasting across the exposed skin of my face was painful.

I was scared of the heather because it's not the sort of thing one can arrest a fall on; I poked at the ground with one trekking pole to see what I could stand on. Higher up, I had to brace against the wind hard enough that the pole bowed out. The slope angle was really uneven, with ice over grass humps and rock steps, and the ice collapsed sometimes, but not others, and while it was not real climbing, it was steep enough that I was on my toes, with my calves burning. Once, when Russ and I were in our early twenties, I fell down this face—not the shoulder, but the chute. I didn't slide, but went head-over-heels for 600 feet through a series of rock bands and blueberry bushes covered with slush. The spinning momentum is the part I really remember. I thought my left arm was broken, and I needed stitches in one knee. Russ was hungry and wanted to stop for Mexican food, so instead of going to the ER we stopped at El Caporal in North Bend. The seating hostess emptied the restaurant's first-aid box trying to patch me up in the ladies' room. Even more than ten years later, every time the crew goes to El Caporal after a mission—usually when the North Bend Bar and Grill is too crowded, so we have to move over a few blocks, and there are fifteen or so of us sitting at all the tables pushed together— she'll still pick me out and ask if I'm okay. I'm always okay, but I like that she has my back.

Russ was now so far ahead of me that I was just following the indent of the toes of his bootprints in the verglas and crushed grass. Eventually, I found a large rock that I could use to brace myself against the wind and put my crampons on. I had to do it while kneeling on my backpack while it bucked in the wind, and the straps cut at the exposed skin on my face, and when I tried to get up again I realized that the wind was too strong, and I was going to have to crawl. It was a first for me. I'd never crawled up Granite before. It felt a little unprofessional, and I was grateful that Russ had gone ahead and no one else had made it up here to see.

I had been feeling risk averse lately. Sometimes, on Saturday mornings at four a.m. when we're getting up to climb, ski, or do whatever that weekend holds, sometimes a little part of me wants to stay home and make pancakes. Take Vivian to the aquarium and watch the translucent mint sea anemones waft in the ocean swell. Caley told me once that the greatest thing he ever taught me was how to be calm in the face of anything. I have so few actual skills that I like to use this one, but every once in a while I just long to be with other calm things, and this was not a calm night.

Base wanted status updates. The wind had forced back the other team that was headed up the ridge. Paul and Jenn were going to wait for us just below tree line for a few hours in case we can find Doug and can get him down that far.

I knew Russ wouldn't want to go farther west off the ridge any more than I did, even though it would be far less windy, because a cornice always forms somewhere over there and we wouldn't be able to see it in the dark until we walked off it. Plus, all the snow that had blown off this ridge had been transported elsewhere; there were wind slabs everywhere around us but on this ridge. I wanted no part of going off it and I was glad I could see Russ's crampon marks headed straight up the ice ahead of me. With the volume on my radio cranked, and the mike clipped inside my hood I could hear Caley trying to call me, but he wasn't going to be able to hear me with the wind, and I needed both palms pressed against the ice, so didn't try to answer. We couldn't call base back until we got nearly to the top, where the angle changes. He tried calling Russ, then he tried calling me again. After a half hour of trying I could hear the tone of his voice change, like he wasn't sure that we were going to answer.

At the top, Russ spent five minutes in a fruitless search for the key, but we'd have to dig through probably ten feet of snow, and the look-out itself was locked and shuttered with plywood covering the door and windows, with a cable lock around the plywood and a padlocked trap door blocking the stairwell, like we knew it would be. Every surface, including the locks, was covered with an inch of black ice, and that was coated with six more inches of white, windblown rime.

We started digging a snow cave twenty feet from the lookout's base. Midnight came when we were halfway through. The entrance was deep enough to shelter the mike, so base could hear us rather than just a rush of wind on the radio. I called down to Caley to wish him a happy New Year. After thirty seconds of silence, during which I assumed Doug was regaining his calm, Ed got on the radio and wished us a happy New Year, too, and then we went back to digging. It was the end of the operational period. Duty change for the deputies. So Ed was headed home. Caley was going to sleep in his car, and Jenn and Paul were headed back down so they could go back to searching at first light. Caley said he'd turn on his radio again at six a.m. Sunrise wouldn't come until 7:45.

I've never understood why people sleep in snow caves for fun, but I do see the practicality of getting out of the wind until daylight. We'd come the length of the distance we thought Doug had traveled. He could have been anywhere, but we thought he would most likely be here. Maybe he was; he could have dug his own snow cave, and would likely not look out until morning. We could be right next to him and not even know it. So we'd wait here for dawn.

Taylor had borrowed my stove a week before, for the first three days we'd spent looking for the skier missing near Kendall Stump, and I had forgotten to get it back. It was rattling around in the back of his car. The stove had been my Mother's Day present from Russ and somehow, even seven months later, I still never had it when I needed it. It remained brand-new.

Taylor was in the parking lot. He radioed that he'd hike up the stove or whatever else we needed, like a tent; but we didn't really need it, we just wished we had it, and it would've taken him the rest of the night to reach us, unless it got any windier. If it got windier, then he'd get blown off the ridge, and even if he didn't, once he showed up we'd only have to make the snow cave bigger because no tent was going to stand up to this. So we said thanks, but best not. It was too bad about the stove, not that there was so much room for it in my pack anyway. My emergency blanket, which hadn't folded up nearly as small as it had in the package ever since the guy at Rattle-snake had used it, seemed to take up half the space.

In the snow cave I emptied out my backpack, crawled in on top of it, arranged my shovel blade as a backrest, and tucked the orange and silver tarp over us. Russ, who was partially on top of me, started snoring within five minutes. He can sleep anywhere, instantly, under any conditions, but I like to leave my headlamp on and not fall asleep on nights when I think I might freeze or get buried alive. I pointed my headlamp up at him. We got engaged less than twenty feet from this spot. Two lines of snot were running from his nose into his mouth. Unlikely to ring in this New Year with a kiss.

It was getting windier, and I spent the rest of the night keeping track of how many inches of spindrift landed on me per hour and, because this was urban-interface-style mountaineering, checking my email and listening to *The Moth*, *Planet Money*, and *Philosophy Talk* podcasts. Well, that and I kept making sure the entrance to the snow cave stayed open.

I don't mind being cold, but lately I have been more upset about being wet. It didn't used to bother me, but now I'm not excited about another cycle of macerated skin, weeks of peeling chunks off my fingers and feet. Under the emergency tarp it must be above freezing because the spindrift was melting; my pumpkin-colored synthetic parka soaked through, and I ended up sitting in a puddle of water on top of Russ's ubiquitous emergency industrial trash bag. In the rush to get out the door I had forgotten my shell pants. I had to pee and spent a while deciding whether, if I just peed in my summer-weight softshell pants, I would get any wetter, or if I really wanted to exit back out into the wind and possibly freeze my lady parts for no real gain.

When it finally came, the predawn was crisp and clear, the wind whipping the snow into a curl over the ridge. We were like surfers teetering on the edge of an ethereal wave. My jacket and pants froze instantly when we left the snow cave, and I couldn't stand up against the wind. Could have no exposed skin in the face of it. The wind forced air into my lungs, and I yelled for Doug—but Russ was right next to me, and even he couldn't hear me.

We crawled along the ridge for a while, but I was afraid of getting blown off. Any footprints here would have been obliterated seconds after they were made.

Then for five minutes everything was a glowing rose as the sun climbed gold over the horizon. It had been cloudy for so long that I'd forgotten this happens, or maybe I thought that a sunrise like this belongs to real mountain ranges, not just foothills beside a major highway, but I guess today the mountain was taking back its identity as a breathtaking force in the universe, and on my knees on the ridge with my ice axe and whippet lodged as firmly as possible, I couldn't help but be attracted to its power.

Caley was back on the radio. "Where can you go safely from where you're at? I want to at least get you guys to look down into East Bowl. But you're up there, so look at it and if you can't do it, you can't."

We said that we would go look at it in the light, now that we could see the snowpack and investigate properly, and we started back down the shoulder.

We didn't know whether Doug had an avalanche beacon. Part of the cornice we'd worried about the night before had fallen—either triggered by a human, or broken off of its own volition—so now we climbed below it into the debris and walked through it, looking for clues. A clue is a hat or a glove, or a hand, or a face in among the blocks. There was nothing. We turned our beacons to receive, and heard nothing.

I didn't want to spend a lot of time looking through debris. Technically, this was the first real day of looking for Doug—I don't think night-time searching really counts—and reason dictates that we don't look for a body the first day. We look for footprints at the bottom of avalanche and cornice debris. We look for a snow cave, we look for sheltered places at the bottom of fall lines. We look for the places someone would go if they were still alive. I look for where I would go, because I know quite a bit about Doug, and read the terrain the same way Doug does, with familiarity and methodical reason. He is a better climber than I am, but maybe all climbers have similar thoughts about how to MacGyver the terrain into helping them.

It got less windy as we got lower; no surprise. We stopped at tree line. My jacket had unfrozen and gone back to being soaked. I wrung it out and put it away, leaving only the bottom five jackets.

I wanted to stay in the thickest trees; the sun was warming the snow, including most of the cornice that still hung above us. We were sinking up above our knees. Russ tried to put his snowshoes on, but all the aged plastic straps cracked off in his hands. Poor timing for gear breakdown, but then, I suppose all things only last so long.

He laughed and said, "I guess I should be grateful that it's been so long since the last time I had to use my snowshoes."

So I kept going downhill, and he post-holed in my snowshoe prints. Search teams were converging around us, and a helicopter that had been circling far above us for the past half hour had just left to refuel.

After another five minutes, we found some avalanche debris in my chosen thickest stands of trees. My friend John from Olympic Mountain Rescue was just to the east of it; we could hear him call in his position from where we stood, slightly lower on the west. Russ asked John if his guys could come over and help us search the debris.

"I'm not sure how old this debris is," I said. "It doesn't look new, but it's hard to tell since there was probably wind ripping through here last night."

"It looks older than a day to me, too," said Russ, "but the cornice debris we were picking through earlier must have fallen yesterday, and that looked degraded too, like the edges were sanded. This could be the same thing."

On his way over to us, John found Doug against a tree in the debris. He saw his red snowshoe from across the ridge. Doug was dead. We were there in five minutes.

One of John's team members worked for Doug. All of us knew him, at least by reputation. The weather was sunny, with a strong and steady breeze. The cornice and wind slabs were still above us, and though it was still freezing in the shade, it wasn't safe to stay long. We sat for a few minutes with Doug, the tree, and the avalanche debris. I didn't have anything to say. There were plenty of people who knew Doug better than I did, and I didn't feel I had the right to sway the thing in any one direction. Sometimes I think the best thing I can do is just be there and say nothing. So I sat there and said nothing.

After a while, one of the guys who'd known Doug wanted a minute, so some of the Olympic Mountain Rescue guys started hiking back down the way they'd come to find the best route out. Russ and I walked the other direction, out from under the canopy into the blinding sunshine where we'd left our packs. We hadn't really eaten much dinner the night before, and now that we had a minute, I was hungry. Or maybe I wasn't hungry, but I thought the act of unwrapping food would give me something to do with my hands until the last team showed up with the litter. Somewhere in my pack, I had a cheese stick and some gummy bears.

I was thinking about one time, when McCall was still a stay-at-home dad, and Aaron was about to leave for residency, when we went on one more search together for a missing state trooper. It turned into a strange Odyssey-like journey; Snohomish County had only asked SMR for three people, which was unusual, and then after we'd driven halfway there, they changed their minds and said they only needed two people, but we said we couldn't leave McCall by the side of the freeway at midnight. Then, when we got to the trailhead, nobody was there except for a single deputy who asked us to hike from the Cascade River Road over to Holden Village. That seemed nuts to us, because it's over thirty miles of snow-covered high mountain pass crossing from the west to the east side of the state. The weather had been completely socked in for days, and we thought there was no way three of us could find one missing guy in all that country, with no visibility. And where was EMRU? They'd asked us to come to their county, but where were they? The deputy didn't know, but he was confident the missing state trooper would hike out on his own any minute, so we weren't going to have to make a more cohesive plan.

Later, it turned out that a team from EMRU had taken a police boat up Lake Chelan and was planning to start hiking from Holden toward us after spending the night in the Lutherans' lodge there and eating a pancake breakfast in sunny eastern Washington. But we thought we were alone. So we started hiking with no cell phone service or radio comms with anyone. Even if the deputy did walk out, there was no way we'd find out for days; but we said we'd do our best to look anyway. We found a cigarette-smoking man by following the orange glow in the dark woods, and what we were pretty sure was a booby-trapped meth lab; we nearly fell to our deaths while side-slipping above a gorge on snowshoes; and we found a lot of cougar tracks and deep snow, but no deputies. It gave us forty-eight hours to discuss our hopes for the future and say goodbye before we finally realized we weren't going to make it anywhere close to Holden. We were running out of cheese and gummy bears, and needed to get home.

But before the deputy did eventually find his way out on his own and return to his family, McCall told me about one of his early trips out with his cousin Doug, up McClellan Butte. There are two avalanche chutes that can be dangerous early in the season. McCall had made it across those, but the top of the peak, on the border with the Cedar River Watershed, is a short, steepish scramble, and there had been a few inches of snow. Then they'd seen the snow start to slide on the rock, and somehow Doug had stopped but McCall hadn't. He fell down the face, hundreds of feet, hitting a lot of trees on the way down, finally stopping when he squarely hit a big one with his face. McCall said he had to flip his own scalp back up on top of his head, and he broke all of his teeth—but, he said, it ended up being okay because his dad was a dentist. Now he always wears safety glasses, because his tear ducts were ripped out during the fall and so his eyes tend to dry out.

When Doug got down to him, he said, "Well, you gonna walk out?" So McCall did. And after some facial and dental reconstruction they went on to have many more adventures together.

So here was another avalanche and another tree, but this time, no walking out. The team with the litter finally arrived, and we wrapped Doug in my orange and silver emergency tarp. I have done this so many times, and if it ever stops feeling like it did the first time, then I'll know it's time to quit.

It's funny, the terms people use for this. Packaging. We packaged the subject. That's not really what we do. We wrapped a death shroud around his body. The kind of death shroud climbers get: A Mylar ultralight silver one. And we carried him out in our arms because it was too windy for a helicopter to try winching, and because I think it means more to walk slowly through the woods, carrying someone by hand while the afternoon sun slants through the trees. It's an unmarked processional, passing a body hand to hand, sometimes ending with a hundred twinkling lights, people standing in the dark, the strange collection of people who come to do this thing. Who want to help—but no one can help, and so we end up carrying the bodies of climbers, again and again.

Base had transformed into a thing unfamiliar; there was a warming tent serving soup, apple fritters, and cheese squares, and a pile of sandwiches on French bread. There was a chaplain wearing ballet flats on the ice. She'd put a pair of dollar-store knit gloves over the toes of her shoes. Her feet must have been freezing. And there were a lot of deputies. Senators had called. The Secretary of the Interior issued a statement. Doug had a lot of friends.

I can't help with grief, the loss of human connection. I'm close enough to see the ties. I can see the loss, but I can't disrupt the story or interact with the characters. Even if I could, I shouldn't; that's not my story to tell. I'm not a real person anyone will remember. I'm just an act of serendipity, or a candle in the window, a nebulous help that came too late. Just someone whispering, "Fair winds and a following sea." It's so funny that I expend so much energy to accomplish so little of what actually matters.

Ed was back on duty, marking yet a new operational period, another deputy shift change. I sat in the command RV and listened to the medical examiner talk on speakerphone to Doug's widow. No one actually needed to talk to me, and it looked like nobody was eating any of the sandwiches—and I hadn't actually eaten anything but some gummy bears since the Chinese food the night before. I took an entire French-loaf-sized sandwich. Doug Caley, Doug McCall, and Doug Walker went home, and then Russ and I went home, too, where we nudged Snowflake, Vivian's stuffed pink seal, off the sofa and moved her new seventy-two-piece art set from Christmas to the floor. We sat on opposite ends of the couch. The couch is old, and the springs have a lot of give, but I like sinking into it; it feels like it's holding me. I tore the sandwich in half. "Happy New Year," I said to Russ, holding out the piece that looked like it had more roast beef on it.

GUYE PEAK

RIGHT NOW, I HAVE TO be a better runner. Larry and Taylor convinced me to run a thirty-mile race with 9,000 feet of elevation gain during my fourth week of nursing school because we need to be faster in the mountains this summer. Because *I* need to be faster.

I have to be faster and I have to keep my head leading unprotectable alpine rock, I have to be able to ski chutes even though I can still remember the faces of the folks who have died falling down them. Plus, it takes work to keep up my certifications—avalanche, medical, swiftwater, technical rigging classes, as well as all the legal, helicopter and crime-scene stuff. Not to mention making time for the actual rescues. I've done sixteen already since January, and it's still only spring, long before the busy season. And I have to run.

Then there's school. My nursing professor, Betty, says that the key is focus. "This is the hardest thing you'll ever do in your life. You need to let go of everything else and concentrate if you want to succeed here."

I've heard those words many times from many people over the years. I'm not sure that it's possible to judge the difficulty of another person's life, to know what will be the hardest thing they'll ever do.

School takes a lot of time, but I suspect there are worse things out there that I'll meet before the end.

I'm not so hubristic to think I totally understand nursing school yet, though, and it's really important that I not fail, lest too many failures in a row label me a poor bet. I need a concrete skill set I can use in the real world.

Anyway, I'm taking Betty's words seriously as a cue to become more capable in general, because I have a lot I'm not willing to let go of. Vivi says she misses me. When I try to leave for the library she cries, wrapped around my leg, and she wants me to sleep in her bed every night. I need to spend more time with her when she's awake. I won't let go of my community, because I spent the first half of my life putting it together—it's my life's work, and it's my greatest source of personal happiness. When I'm separated from my community I become sadder, and less productive. I know it's selfish, but I will not be unwedged.

I thought it was a choice to help people, but—psych!—it's not. For a long time I tried to mitigate when the texts came through; I tried to be good and stay home, spend quality time watching TV with Russ, clean the kitchen, finish the extra credit, go on vacations like normal people, but I realized that most of the time it doesn't make me happy. So now I know that, when the next big rescue comes, even though I need to stay in the back corner of the library making flash cards for osteo-arthritis drugs, then go home and make dinner, and then go back to the library—when my friends call me because they need help, there'll just be a trail of index cards on the carpet leading out the door.

Friends are what I want more than anything for Vivian, too. She made a friend at school and wanted to have her over for a playdate on the last Friday in May, a week before finals for my first quarter of nursing school. I was nervous about spending the evening anywhere but the library, but Vivian's in second grade and this was the first time that she's wanted to have a girl over to our house. So it was a big deal. She'd talked about it for a week, planned it out. First she and Diana would dress up our two new kittens in doll clothes—the fish had finally died and, in a show of benevolence which he later regretted, Russ let two fluffy-eared kittens join our little household. Then Vivi and Diana would make friendship bracelets, eat popsicles, and lie down together in the hammock in the backyard. I can't help doubting that the hammock part will work out: it's going to rain. The weather has been cold and wet for days. But I want to make the rest of it awesome.

Then on Friday morning I get a text that two German tourists, a father and son, have failed to return from a day hike they started the day before, trying to get to Mason Lake, just west of Granite Mountain. Right now at Mason Lake it's all patchy snow, fog, and rain in dense forest, dripping with black and lime-green lichen. I heard the rain pounding all last night, could see the water running down the black dirt when I closed my eyes. I could see how it would be pretty easy to get lost in those conditions. But I can't go look for them. Someone else will have to go this time.

I take Vivian to school, and then go to class in Seattle. On Fridays I'm done at 1 p.m., one hour before Vivian gets out of Carnation Elementary. I have to wear my running shoes to class so I can sprint across campus and down the hill to my car behind Sears, and make it through every yellow light, or else Vivian will be the last kid standing at parent pickup, drenched, with the staff watching for me through the window. I know what that feels like to worry that your mom might have forgotten you, especially when a new friend is coming over for a first playdate.

By midafternoon, someone finds the father and son. One of them is injured, and they're stuck on a boulder field above Lake Kulla Kulla. Carrying someone out on the trail from Mason Lake isn't too bad, but it looks like these hikers overshot Mason Lake and did an additional forty-five minute bushwhack through dense undergrowth to Kulla Kulla. They're now on the far side of the lake after scrambling even farther up toward Mount Defiance. It takes a lot of people and effort to pass someone hand-to-hand down boulder fields, and, once they get back to tree line, to carry a litter forward while pressing against a wall of brush. It's slow going and everyone gets really scratched up. Then from Mason Lake, it's still roughly five more miles to the trailhead. I get text after text pleading for more people to help carry the injured man out.

Russ leaves work to go help. Normally, he would watch Vivi when he got home so I could go study at the library, but tonight nothing is going to keep me from hosting this playdate. With Russ going on the rescue, I feel less guilty for not going myself.

An hour later, I'm making matching sorbet-colored friendship bracelets. The girls originally wanted fancy ones, where the colors make flower patterns, but it turned out the pattern was significantly complex, so Vivi asked me to make them instead. Since then they've been busy making the kittens fall asleep on their backs, and then watching their legs and whiskers twitch.

My phone beeps. It's a new rescue. They need more people for both the old one and the new one. The new one is for a stuck hiker on Kaleetan Peak, one valley to the west of the Alpental Valley across from Chair Peak. It's the second mission there in less than a week—I pulled an all-nighter there four nights ago. We climbed up a snow-choked gully at twilight, not sure whether it was the right gully because it was so foggy. We checked the top of the peak, yelled for the missing man, peered over the sheer cliff down the backside but saw nothing, and then post-holed back out in the dark and increasingly heavy rain, and handed off our assignment to the next team. I had to leave the search to go home, pick up my scrubs, print out my homework, and leave for my clinical rotation by 4 a.m. The hiker walked out eventually; he'd made it off the peak, but then got turned around and wandered the wrong way down toward the Middle Fork. When he finally found his way back out he told Steve he'd seen apparitions of Native Americans ahead of him in the snow, and he'd followed them for a while.

Russ calls me to say that he got diverted on his way to Lake Kulla Kulla to get the stuck hiker at Kaleetan. He's going to hike in with McCall. I told him it's a little sketchy right now because the slabs above Melakwa Lake are melting out. There's nothing but air under the white fingers that reach up from the lake. You can watch the water run down the rock, into slimy moats that smell like acrid black moss, stagnant cavernous space, and small, grey, floating moths, at least if you get your face down close enough. "Be careful," I say, pulling tight but not too hard on the final knots of a two-dimensional orange sorbet flower.

I take Vivian's friend Diana home at dinnertime, and call Russ again to see how it's going. He says it's fine, he found the Kaleetan guy in the fog wandering down near the base of the route, and he and McCall are about to start heading back to the trailhead.

"Did it go okay with Diana?" I ask Vivi. "So fun." says Vivi. "Can we have Diana and Diana's sister Daisy over next week?"

I try to focus on parenting even though I can't turn off the siren in my brain that's singly focused on the direness of my homework situation, and my suspicion that my crew will be going out to dinner now, sharing stories and generally bonding, and I'm going to miss it. But I haven't spent any special mother-daughter time with Vivi in a month, so we decide to go out for Indian food to celebrate her making a new friend, and now possibly two friends if we have Daisy over next week, too. I'll just stay up a little later doing homework after she goes to bed.

As Vivi and I walk into Kanishka Indian Cuisine for shahi paneer and spinach naan, I get a text for a third rescue. This one is for a man stuck on Guye Peak, a rocky outcrop next to Mount Snoqualmie, just across from the Alpental Ski area. Russ calls and says they're going to try to get the wet and somewhat scratched up guys from Kaleetan and Kulla Kulla to head over to Guye Peak once they've finished their respective rescues because there's some sort of traffic nightmare farther west on I-90. Even though they could use fresh people, nobody can get through to the pass. Ed is trying to get cars to line up on the freeway shoulder at Exit 47, and he'll send a police escort to get them up to the pass, but nobody's sure if that's going to happen. "Okay," I say, "be careful and good luck."

Back at home, once Vivi's asleep, I sit down to write a nursing process paper, and don't look up until I realize that Russ isn't home yet at 1:00 a.m. I didn't really expect that he would be back any earlier, but now I wonder how it's going. I step out onto our front porch to stretch and listen to the rain hitting the strawberry plants, each drop landing with a distinctive splat on large leaves and rock-hard white fruit. I call Russ again.

"Well," he says, "we tried going up a number of gullies on the south side of Guye, but we couldn't find the right one in the dark. You just get blinded by the light of your own headlamp bouncing off the damn fog right in front of your face. And it's raining like being stuck in a washing machine on the cold cycle, and we didn't want to get too far up any gully without knowing it was the right one because all the rock up there is friable crap."

"So what's the plan?" I ask.

"I was going to stay up there, but I'm tired and my feet have been wet for too long," says Russ. He wants me to switch him out, says the plan is to try again at first light. He'll be home in an hour and I need to start up the pass as soon as he gets back home to Vivi in order for me to get to the command post and organized while it's still dark. Caley and McCall are staying in base. Caley'll be on the radio. I'll run Field Ops.

"Okay," I say. "Russ, why is McCall staying in base?"

"He says he won't set foot on Guye," says Russ. "He says it tried to kill him, says that the rock quality is appalling, which is true. I don't know what the story is."

I think that's a lot coming from McCall, who had his face crushed in that avalanche on McClellan Butte a few years ago, and whose cousin died on Granite five months ago—but he'll go back to both of those places.

I'm not tired. I haven't actually been tired for a while. It's a strange thing, but I'm grateful. At first I used to just feel this way when I was climbing at night. If I was cold enough I wouldn't get sleepy, which made it easier to keep going—some primal part of my brain just flipped a survival-mode switch and turned off sleepiness. Now I feel like I have more in common with old people with respiratory diseases; they can't sleep because they can't breathe, hypoxia leads to agitation, and it's really hard to sleep and panic at the same time. I think this is something similar, the weight of so much to do pushing down on my chest flips that switch again and I can pull one or two all-nighters a week, keep it rolling day after day. I don't even drink coffee. I'm always already awake when my alarm goes off.

"There's leftover Indian—that thing with cheese chunks in the fridge," I tell Russ as he walks through the front door directly to the laundry room, leaving a trail of water and pine needles. "Where's base?" I ask, following him through the kitchen.

"Snow Lake." Russ throws a wad of raingear and the rest of his clothes into the dryer.

"Is there any snow up there?"

"No."

"Is—" I start, but he's closed the bathroom door.

I walk back into the living room, where my laptop glows blue in the dark. I take a deep breath and exhale completely while closing the screen; feel myself leaving. It's not sleep, but it's like rest, going out the door, driving through the night, a tiny dry capsule in a world saturated with water, hurtling toward my best friends in the world.

I love the cold. I love the struggle, the realness, the ridiculousness, and the tenderness of it. Rescue missions are not actually work, not a career; money, power, and prestige mean nothing out here. It's not a vocation, it's an avocation. I don't know why it took me so long to find the words to hold it up against. This is just what I do for love, just taking the time to be with someone who needs someone to be with them. I'm working on the career stuff, but for a few minutes I need it to be just us, standing together in the dark.

There's nobody in the Snow Lake parking lot. It takes me half an hour of driving around to find everyone parked in a residential neighborhood turnaround at the end of a spur road half a mile away. The county van with the flood light illuminates the rain. Behind it, a few quiet, hardy homeowners sit huddled around a bonfire, drinking at 3 a.m. on a Saturday morning in May, their houses bright with white party lights.

I feel an almost manic happiness. I want to breathe in the smoke from the fire and this coldest kind of metallic mountain rain, the dustiness of moths zapped in the blinding floodlight under the RV's awning, and remember it all together. Hold onto the feeling when I have to go back. I can taste my own gratefulness to be here. I feel drunk on it, and I have to lean against Caley's car to refocus. The slight jar causes water to run down the condensation-fogged window. Caley is probably asleep in the back seat, and just got dripped on.

McCall's sitting alone in the van, staring at a photocopy of a photo of Guye Peak marked up with a highlighter.

"Hey," I say. As soon as I see him I realize that I haven't seen McCall since we put together a dinner at Larry's house with the hopes of decompressing a little bit after finding his cousin Doug's body in the avalanche back in January. Or maybe I saw him at the memorial service after that. But it's been a while. I'm glad he's here.

McCall looks sleepy. Caley lurches into the truck looking sleepy, too. I must have woken him up. I love the way people look when they just wake up. Sure, they're blurry and puffy, but it's so nice to be with people who don't care what they look like. I laugh because they're so disheveled, and they laugh because I'm laughing, because they don't know why I'm laughing. Ninety percent of the energy in the van is mine.

"So this guy," I say, "where is he exactly? What's the story?"

"Okay," says McCall, "this is for a fire fighter paramedic who thought he was hiking Mount Snoqualmie, but he made a wrong turn and ended up on Guye instead. Then, instead of going back down the way he came up, he tried hiking down the shoulder and ended up downclimbing pretty close to the middle of the face, about a third of the way down, where he finally realized he was stuck and called 911. He's says he's a climber and a parkour expert. I guess that must have helped him get there, because he's in a tough spot."

There is a brief pause while McCall reaches for, and then sadly shakes his empty coffee mug, and while I watch him do it I examine my feelings about rescuing fire fighters. This is not my first one, but I feel the same about this one as the others: I don't mind rescuing him as long as he's okay being rescued by me. And so far, every fire fighter I've rescued has capitulated when it's come down to me, or death. They probably don't go home and tell their buddies about it, but you can't blame them for that.

"Yeah," says Caley, "so we were out looking at the face earlier, Ed had the dude on speakerphone, and the dude was pretty casual about it, and Ed tells him to turn his phone's flashlight on so we can see if we can find him with the spotting scope. He does, and all the guys who were standing around base were like, 'Oh, shit' at the same time, and I'm not sure Ed muffled his phone fast enough. The guy was a little more subdued after that."

Guye Peak is right next to Alpental. The man is stuck in the middle of the biggest obvious face directly above the parking lot. But even though it's not way in the backcountry, the place is notorious for imposing rescuer difficulty. The rock quality is crap. Anchors are scarce. All our ropes get hung up on the weirdly angular rock and tiny roots that reach out like gnarled fingers from the black moss that grows in the cracks. Large sections of it are not quite vertical, just steep ledges covered in black moss nine inches thick. The weather is frequently absolute shit, and fog hangs in the basin even when it isn't raining. But now it is raining.

"He kept calling periodically, but his phone died a couple hours ago," says McCall. "He's on a tiny ledge holding onto a scrub tree. He doesn't have a backpack, he's wearing sweatpants, and the snow line has come down. He said he was soaked and it had started snowing pretty hard the last time we talked. Although, he has one of those emergency bracelets made out of parachute cord. Ed told him to unravel it, and use it to tie himself to the scrub tree in case he passes out."

"Don't people untie themselves from stuff when they get super hypothermic?" asks Caley.

"Maybe his hands will get frozen enough that he won't be able to untie himself?" I say.

"You have a better suggestion you could have contributed?" asks McCall, starting to wave his arms around in exasperation.

"Nah," I say, "let's just go get him."

McCall says that the rest of the crew is either asleep in their cars, trying to dry their gear on their bodies, or else they've briefly gone home to put their raingear in the dryer and eat some food in lieu of sleeping, but everybody should all be back in the next few minutes. They've also called Everett, Tacoma, and Olympic mountain rescue for reinforcements, although nobody is sure who will come; we've been asking for help a lot lately, and if anyone does come they'll have a long drive ahead of them.

"There's food here, anyhow," says McCall. "The homeowners brought us hot dogs to roast on the bonfire . . . but those might actually be gone. And then there's some amazing rice pudding in a crock pot next to the bumper. It's probably cold now, though."

"Y'think?!" says Caley. "Actually, it's probably just as good cold for breakfast. It has raisins in it."

McCall nods, looking serious. "I think there are some bowls left somewhere."

I leave them to manage base operations and keep praying that the gas station will open soon so they can get coffee.

I find Patrick, and tell Caley that Team 1 is leaving. "Do good work, Bree," says Caley, and we head up the steep rocky trail to Cave

Ridge, where we'll cut over to the North Peak of Guye. Around the time the trail fully disappears under hard crusty snow, it starts to get light and I start kicking steps; my approach shoes have a harder edge than Patrick's trail runners. An ice axe would have been useful, but I guess it was one less thing to carry. Rain is still falling through the fog. We're hiking in all our raingear. I usually get too sweaty to wear full raingear and hike as fast as I can at the same time, but this morning's cold.

Larry and Nick head up behind us. Two more guys offered to help them schlep the obscene amount of rigging gear I've requested at least as far as the top of the north summit—they don't feel comfortable going farther, since they are still soaking wet and tired from last night, and they aren't up for rock climbing in the pouring rain.

So we've got Patrick, Larry, Nick, and me, plus two volunteers from OMR named Landis and Kaster sent by Caley and McCall to try to find their way up the South Gully. Between us, we need to access the fire fighter from one side of the peak or the other, because no one else is coming. Caley says he'll send out another request for more help, but folks are already tired, and a lot are out of town because it's the beginning of a three-day weekend, which I'd forgotten.

"Don't expect anyone else," he says. "You going to be okay?"

I think about it. Patrick has been out all night. So have Nick and Larry. I'm thinking about a line from *Fight Club:*

> *You are not your job, you're not how much money you have in the bank. You are not the car you drive. You are not the contents of your wallet. You are not your fucking khakis. You are the all singing, all dancing crap of the world.*

"Caley," I say.

"Yeah."

"I could use some more people, but I think I'm doing really good, actually."

I fix a line to the south summit, have to take off my gloves to climb it. It's only Class 4, but my pack is insanely heavy and two inches of slush cover the slabs, obscuring holds, overlaying slick black mud and last year's rotten vegetation. I worry because Larry and Nick have to make it up from the north summit across to the higher south one with—I'm not sure how much weight in rope and kit they're carrying— as much as it is possible to make upward progress with. It's really hard to keep your center of gravity over your toes with that much weight pulling you backward. I belay Nick up last, and when he gets to the top he sits down in the snow. I can see his legs are shaking, and as I keep looking his knees turn white in only a few seconds, the snow is falling so fast. "That was slimy," I say.

Patrick is putting on all the spare clothing he has while eating the world's smallest package of fish crackers. "I got them on an airplane," he says. "I didn't have any food to put in my pack and they were sitting on the counter."

"Nice," I say. "Did you try any of the rice pudding? None of you guys got any dinner last night, did you?"

But it's too cold to stop here. "Okay," I say to get folks moving again, "let's go."

While they struggle back into standing positions, I can't help thinking that while we've had days when the crew has been less ragged, they actually perform better the harder the job is. I can tell they're just getting started.

About eleven in the morning, Landis and Kaster think they have voice contact from the south ridge. By then they're only about 200 feet below us, and we meet up just below the top of the north summit. But once we're together, we can't hear anything more from the fire fighter down on the face, even after we yell together repeatedly leaning out over the edge. But we think that if Landis heard him, and the guy managed to yell back, even just once, that's a pretty good sign that he's still alive.

"Hey, Kaster," I say, "can you rappel down over the edge a ways? If you can get eyes on him, you could direct us to the spot on the ridge directly above where he's at, and then we can go snag him."

"Really?" says Larry, "Sticking the Olympic guys with prusiking back up their rope while we go hog the glory job of actually rescuing the guy?!? Nice. Way to play well in the sandbox."

"Okay," I say, laughing. "One of us can do it." Then, narrowing my eyes at him, "So you wanna?"

But then Patrick says he'll go. Because Landis thinks the fire fighter sounded like he was some distance below us, we tie off one end of our longest rope, a 300-foot static line, and Patrick rappels over the edge.

After five minutes, Patrick radios to say he's pretty close to directly above the guy, and he thinks he can retrieve him. I look over at the OMR guys and shrug, and they shrug, and very diplomatically confirm that we did try to give them glory jobs. Then we all stand around waiting for Patrick, and the snow turns back into rain.

Patrick calls again. "It's looking good, but my rope isn't going to be long enough."

"Give us a minute," I say, "we'll tie our second 300-foot rope onto the end of the first one and lower you."

Soon Larry and Nick are at the anchor lowering Patrick. Nick calls over that they're at the end of the second 300-foot rope.

"Hey, Patrick," I call over the radio, looking down over the edge where I can't see a thing. "Are you there yet?"

"Really close," says Patrick, "but not quite."

We stand in a huddle and discuss what to do. We're out of 300-foot static ropes, but we do have a couple of climbing ropes. One we'd used to build an anchor extension, but we had one left.

Climbing ropes are designed to be light enough to carry in the alpine, and they're high-stretch so that when a climber falls, she won't break her back by suddenly getting jerked to a stop. But more weight equates to more stretch, and the force required to pull up on a climbing rope with a two person load ends up being a bit like trying to lift a heavy book with a stretchy rubber band. Every time we have to stop the raise to reset the haul system, Patrick and the fire fighter are going to bounce—a lot—as the amount of force on the rope changes. Then when we start pulling again, it's going to cause yet another change in the force and they'll bounce some more. A climbing rope is strong enough to withstand the force of us pulling two people up. One climber can generate even more force when they take a lead fall during the normal course of climbing. But dealing with the stretch makes the haul much less efficient, and, well, the boinging effect while constantly having to reset with the weight of two people can be both super annoying for the attendant trying to keep their footing, and dangerous because the rope can saw over sharp edges as it stretches back and forth.

Patrick and the fire fighter can't just keep rappelling down to the bottom; we've tried it on previous rescues, but Guye Peak has proven to be too loose and horrible, worse the lower we got. None of us are willing to do that again. We're going to have to raise them back up to the ridgeline and find another way down. But this raise isn't always vertical, and it's bouncy, which means there's a lot of potential for the rope to knock down rocks the size of baseballs or even basketballs, blowing past them like the stars do in *Spaceballs* when the ship goes to ludicrous speed. A rock could cut the rope, or just as easily hit Patrick on the head, and no helmet can stop the big ones. Even if we avoid the rockfall, with the friction of the rope rubbing against the rock, the five of us might not have the strength to actually lift both men. But if we did have the power, a knot in the rope could easily jam under a rock somewhere, and if we kept pulling, the forces could overload the system, leading to catastrophic failure—and then Patrick and the fire fighter would fall a thousand feet down to the talus. Normally for res-cue work, we'd have two larger-diameter low-stretch rescue ropes in parallel for abrasion resistance, to reduce the stretch and in case one cut, not just one long line of ropes tied together in series. But we just couldn't have carried any more rope. So we have to be careful now.

Patrick calls on the radio again. "Hey Bree . . . I'm a little bit wor-ried about rockfall cutting the rope or cutting loose and landing on me. Plus, I'm wondering if you guys have enough mechanical advan-tage to actually get us back up."

"Well," I say, "we sent the guy with the master's in mechanical engineering over the edge, so . . . we'll try our best, but we're going to keep lowering you to the subject and see how bad things are with him, and then let's decide."

We're not sure whether, once we get the fire fighter off the face, we'll be able to walk him out or if we'll have to carry him down. I don't want to go back down the way we came up; especially if we have to carry him out. There aren't great anchors for lowering someone down, no good cracks to put in gear for protection, and it's very diffi-cult to raise and lower a litter along knife-edge ridgelines. Plus, once we make it off Guye Peak itself, the trail out from Cave Ridge is a nasty one for carrying someone; everything below snow line involves walking on large boulders and pushing through slide alder.

I ask the OMR guys what they think about going back out the way they came in, down the South Gully, and they say that while they can't recommend it, it would mostly be rappels, so at least we could keep the subject tied to something.

When Patrick finally makes it down to the fire fighter, we have only enough rope left to make the world's tiniest 9:1 raising system: we'll have to pull nine feet of rope for every foot we raise them. We stand there, looking at it.

"It's a good thing Patrick is very skinny," says Nick.

"Yes, and he only ate fish crackers for breakfast," I add. We all nod solemnly.

I call Caley again to see if anyone can bring us more gear for a two-rope system, or just come to help pull, or even bring bivy gear and food in case we opt to wait out the weather.

"I'm just now able to field another team," he says. "It's three guys. I don't know them. It'll be hours before they get to you—if they make it at all, and they don't have any overnight gear."

"Nice. Thanks, Doug," I say.

"You're welcome, Bree," says Caley. "Is it raining or snowing up there right now? Gotta tell you, it's really warm here in the van."

There are more ESAR teams at base, except they don't have the skill to climb the route in these conditions. But they do have cookies, and they say they'll save us some. We ask for a weather check: the forecast is stormy with heavy rain and fog for at least another forty-eight hours, with no potential for air support to either winch or drop gear for us.

I communicate all of this to Patrick. He says that it's darn cold where he is. Given the other options, he consents to getting raised back up again. He has unintentionally traversed somewhat to climber's right while we were lowering him, and now when the rope comes taut, he realizes that the line isn't plumb. He very briefly thinks he can hold the two of them steady with his foot, but half a second later he and the fire fighter skitter across the face toward an open-book corner. Later, Patrick will say that he knew it was his job to stay between the fire fighter and the rock. So Patrick slams into the corner with his head and his left arm. At first he thinks his arm is broken, and his fingers go numb, but later his head hurt worse than his arm.

It takes four and a half hours to raise Patrick and the fire fighter back up. It is the longest raise I have ever done. There's nothing we can do but pull on the rope as hard as we can, all together. Larry insists that he needs to sit down to pull if he's going to do it for half a day, so it'll be closer to the same motion he uses on his rowing machine. At least we aren't cold anymore.

For the first hour Patrick thinks that it's going to be okay. By the fourth hour of dangling in his harness, being buffeted around in the wind and soaked from both the top and the bottom, he calls back up and says that we need to get our rewarming stuff in order before they reach the top.

I say, "I hear ya, Patrick, we're on it." But we actually can't do any of that because the only thing we can do is keep pulling on the end of the rope and sprinting back to the anchor, then pulling on the rope again.

Nick, the OMR guys, and I keep going around in this tiny circle, pulling rope and creating a trench in the snow as we go.

"I really hope we don't jam a knot," says Nick as we pass each other for the hundredth time.

"Yup," I say.

By late afternoon, I can see Patrick and the fire fighter down below us. An interminable time later they finally make it back up to the rim, and gingerly sit down together at the edge. Because of the 9:1 system, we've pulled over 6,000 feet of rope, and I find myself momentarily upset that the size of the rope piles don't reflect this somewhat herculean effort.

I've bought another space blanket, since my last one left with the ME and Doug. This new one is still tightly folded in its original packaging. I hesitate for a second and then pull it out. Nick fires up the stove to make hot drinks, but then we realize that we haven't brought any tea or soup or anything. We think about squeezing energy gel into the water, but then Larry says that he has some Crystal Lite. Then we make fun of Larry for even owning that. When Nick finally finishes his concoction, it's pink and has a two-inch twig floating in it, and nobody wants to drink it, so we give it to Patrick to use as a hot water bottle.

His arm is sorta working again. I sit down next to him. "Can I look at it?" I ask.

"I don't even really want to look at it," says Patrick.

"Do you feel like you're going to throw up?" He says no.

I want to know, "Are you going to be able to rappel? Can you hold onto stuff?"

"It's fine, whatever, go away," says Patrick.

"How many fingers?" I ask, holding up the middle one.

The fire fighter is fit and in his early twenties. He's really cold, but in amazingly good shape considering that he spent the night on a tiny ledge in a blizzard wearing a windbreaker and sweatpants while tied to a tree with parachute cord. I'm grateful that his legs look like they'll keep working, and we won't have to carry him out.

He's lucky, and he's a cool guy. Tired, though, because anyone would be. He's sitting down on a slush-covered rock, staring into space.

"You did good," I say, crouching next to him. "How long have you been a fire fighter?"

"Almost a year," he says.

"So," I say, "getting to the top is only halfway out. Getting home is still going to take a long time. I know that you must be tough, mentally and physically, to do your job, so I know you can hold it together until we get back to the parking lot." Today he's not in the firehouse. Today, he's in my house, where everyone is treated as equals with empathy, humor, and universal positive regard.

"Yeah, I got this," he says.

"Cool beans," I tell him, "let's rock it out!" I hold out my fist to do the fist-bump thing because I'm all about fist-bumping people right now. The other ladies in nursing school are just going to have to give in, sooner or later.

Then we pack up and start looking for the OMR guys' route down. It's late afternoon. Caley calls to say that he's handing off base to Russell and going home for a few hours. I figure Russ must have dropped Vivi off with my mom.

Fortunately, the three guys Caley sent up pop over the rim just then and guide us back down to the start of the rappels. They have preset anchors running down the gully and brought the ropes I needed earlier.

But that leaves us with ten people—Patrick we're still watching—and we have to lower the fire fighter. He's a climber, but only in the gym, he's never rappelled before, and we have a ton of gear and all those ropes to carry. And as it turns out, the rockfall is so bad that only one person can rappel at a time.

It gets dark and my climbing rope gets stuck on only the second or third rap down. Larry calls down to say that it won't pull and I tell him to leave it, because this is everyone's second night without sleep and without eating anything besides fish crackers and the Crystal Lite that Larry is still surreptitiously adding to his water bottle—well, nobody's eaten anything except me, because I went out for Indian food.

And I've been thinking that we still have way more than enough rope to get down, using the rescue ropes. But it turns out that fat 300-foot ropes don't pull very well, either. The first one gets stuck; the second two pull, but send loads of rocks down, and there isn't really anywhere for the crew down below to get out of the way. I call base again, and Russ says I could just fix all the ropes if I was sure we could make it to the bottom. Normally, we would center the middle of the rope at the anchor, and rap down using both ends; then once we were down, we'd pull on one end of the rope and it would slide through the anchor and come loose so we could use it again. But instead, we can tie the bitter end of the rope to the anchor and rap the whole length of the rope. We could go twice the distance with each rap that way, but we couldn't get the ropes back. We'd have to leave them.

And I remember that's what we ended up doing the last time there was a rescue on Guye; we just came back a couple days later to clean up all of our stuff in daylight, when it wasn't raining and we weren't trying to save someone. And maybe leaving tons of rope doesn't look real professional, but it is still the safest idea, because it's midnight again. I just hope I've calculated the distance right and we won't run out of rope before we get to the bottom.

So we fix almost 1,400 feet of rope. When we can finally see the headlamps of the folks with the cookies below us on the boulder field, I realize that I'm one rope-length short. I radio up to Nick and

Patrick, who are rapping last and so are still the farthest up the drainage, to tell them that they can't tie off the top rope. They need to be able to pull it and bring it down with them, even if that means that Nick has to downclimb part of it, or find something to use as an intermediate anchor.

"Great," says Nick over the radio, "I could use a challenge. I was getting bored up here."

I do actually have one other rope. It's the rope we used as our anchor extension during the really long haul. And I would use it except that, right in the middle of the rope, where despite our best efforts it must have been rubbing on a rock, it had started to abrade. Now it has a lengthy core shot in it. We try duct taping it, but looking at it now, it's bad enough that I'm not going to rap on it without isolating the core shot by tying a knot in the middle of the rope. But by this point I'm rappelling with the fire fighter, and he doesn't actually love rappelling, especially in the dark when he can't see where he's going, so I just don't want to have to mess with passing it.

But then the highest rope pulls for Nick, so we don't have to, and we make it down to the boulder field where we run into ESAR. They give us oatmeal raisin cookies, and escort us back to base.

A friend of the fire fighter's comes to pick him up, says he gets himself into crazy situations all the time, but somehow he always manages to come out of them without a scratch. The fire fighter has finally warmed up, and he is perfectly fine otherwise. His friend must be right. They say thanks and goodbye.

I sit in the command van, waiting to make sure everyone else makes it out, my pants steaming slightly next to the truck's heater. Patrick, Larry, and Nick are still stuck a couple pitches up, watching the rain blow around in the circle of their headlamps, sitting in the rain, waiting for everybody else to get down. Ed has been back in base to work a shift, and then gone home again. Pete is running base now, and Russ is still on the radio.

"You've got to try some of this rice pudding one of the homeowners made us," Russ says. "It's amazing. It's probably cold by now, but you can stick it in the microwave."

"Any chance you can get me some?" I ask, and Russ goes out and comes back in with a red plastic bowl, and jams it in the microwave.

"You can't microwave plastic," says Pete, pulling it back out again and looking through cabinets. "Ah, paper plates." He scrapes the congealed rice pudding onto a paper plate and turns on the microwave, waits thirty seconds, and then hands it to me.

"Thanks, guys," I say.

And I wait for the rest of the crew to come back. I know they're happy—exhausted and kind of beat up, dodging rocks, eating oatmeal cookies, and hacking their way down through the slide alder, but happy. I need to finish my paper today, and work on my flashcards. And I needed to pick Vivi up from my mom's. Then Vivi and I needed to go out for cupcakes and talk about what she wants to do for her eighth birthday party. And I know that there will be another rescue that night, but—maybe it's just the raisins in the rice pudding—but it all tastes sweet.

ACKNOWLEDGMENTS

I WANT TO THANK DEBBIE Anschell, Greg Anschell, Jan Loewen, and Gordon Loewen for welcoming my dulcet dove with open arms every time I foist her on you with no notice. You take my child even when she is sticky, petulant, and you had preexisting dinner plans. I am not sure how many climbers, hikers, runners, and skiers owe their lives directly to your generosity in this matter, but I know that it is a lot.

Also, thanks to my husband Russell for putting up with yet another one of my projects. I know you didn't want me to write another book, but you suffered through it anyway because you knew I really wanted it. Thanks. I promise I'll get a real, paying job soon.

I also want to thank Kate Rogers, Editor in Chief of Mountaineers Books for responding positively to the ludicrous drunken midnight email that I sent suggesting that I should totally write another book while in nursing school; you enable big girls with big dreams. Thanks to Kirsten Colton for being a truly phenomenal developmental editor. Also much gratitude to my project editor Mary Metz and my copyeditor Carol Poole.

Also thanks to the SMR crew present and alumni: Steve Allen, John Angulo, Russ Anschell, Forrest Barker, Paul Bongaarts, Patrick

Brewer, Ben Brown, Garth Bruce, Taylor Brugh, Doug Caley, Jenn Carter, Larry Colagiovanni, Bob Coleman, Nick Constantine, Wes Cooper, Rich Evans, Geoff Ferguson, Drew Fletcher, Jim Gellman, Nathan Greenland, Karl Hangartner, Cheri Higman, Jarek Jaroslaw, Heather Kosaka, Yogesh Kumar, Gretchen Lentz, Andrei Maksimenka, Doug McCall, Derek Newbern, Matt Palubinskas, Dave Perkins, Jim Pitts, Greg Prothman, Imran Rahman, Bob Ricker, Rick Samona, Keith Schultz, Doug Seitz, Gordon Smith, Scott Staton, Sarah Stephan, and also Seth Brothers, Dave Burdick, Ryan Cross, Bill Davis, Doug Daniell, Al Errington, Art Farsh, Doug Hutton, Ryan Lurie, Jonah Manning, Dave Rusho, Stephanie Schiller, Todd Stone, Darby Summers, Warren Thompson, Jessica Todd, Matt Wetzel, John Wick, Ryan Wopshall, Gene Yore, Gary Yngve, Aaron Zabriskie, and so, so many others.

Also thanks to all the usual partners in crime: Ed Christian and Pete Linde from the King County Sheriff's Office, the ESAR crew, most especially Eric Rosenberg, Matt Cosand, Mark Chapman, Paul Macaree, Darren Emmons, Scott MacColman, Nick Menyhard, Kevin Watson, and my early formative influences Jim Lomax, Cheryl Drevecky, Brianna Hartzell, and Julie Wartes—Julie was the best Course II partner ever. Also thanks to BARK, SPART, 4X4, Darian, Ty, Don, Mark, and the rest of Watershed Protection, OMR, TMR, EMR and the HRT team, all the rangers at MORA, and anyone who ventured out on foot from Medic 1 when we asked for help, and thanks to Eastside Fire and Rescue and Bellevue Fire for character development.

My eternal gratitude also goes to Ted Cox, the greatest raconteur who ever lived. I miss you. To Amanda Casari for reading my early drafts, Corki Budnick, Betty Kost, Anna Shanks, Sue Christenson, Patti Kwok, Lori Stephens, and Lisa Zerby for reminding me that the world is full of kind professionals, and everyone at Evergreen Hospice—hugs to the volunteers who make the coffee and refill the candy dishes. I know what you really do.

GLOSSARY

AED	Automated External Defibrillator
BARK	Backcountry Avalanche Rescue K9
EMRU	Everett Mountain Rescue Unit
EMT	Emergency Medical Technician
ESAR	Explorer Search and Rescue
IFMGA	International Federation of Mountain Guides Associations
ITOL	In Town Operations Leader
KCSO	King County Sheriff's Office
LODD	Line of Duty Death
MRA	Mountain Rescue Association
OMR	Olympic Mountain Rescue
PMR	Portland Mountain Rescue
SAR	Search and Rescue
SMR	Seattle Mountain Rescue
TMR	Tacoma Mountain Rescue

ABOUT THE AUTHOR

BREE LOEWEN IS A PAST training chair and a current board member for Seattle Mountain Rescue. She has helped hundreds of injured climbers, skiers, and other outdoor enthusiasts who ran into misfortune in the Cascade mountains over the better part of two decades. During those years she also spent time as an EMT for a private ambulance company, a climbing ranger on Mount Rainier, full-time mom, volunteer fire fighter, secretary for her daughter's co-op preschool, volunteer fire chaplain, watershed inspector, hospice volunteer, paramedic student, city planning board member, school-bus driver, and nursing student. Bree has written for *Rock and Ice* and *Alpinist* magazines. In her spare time she goes climbing, then comes home and bakes fruit pies. This is her second book.

recreation • lifestyle • conservation

MOUNTAINEERS BOOKS is a leading publisher of mountaineering literature and guides—including our flagship title, *Mountaineering: The Freedom of the Hills*—as well as adventure narratives, natural history, and general outdoor recreation. Through our two imprints, Skipstone and Braided River, we also publish titles on sustainability and conservation. We are committed to supporting the environmental and educational goals of our organization by providing expert information on human-powered adventure, sustainable practices at home and on the trail, and preservation of wilderness.

The Mountaineers, founded in 1906, is a 501(c)(3) nonprofit outdoor activity and conservation organization whose mission is "to explore, study, preserve, and enjoy the natural beauty of the outdoors." One of the largest such organizations in the United States, it sponsors classes and year-round outdoor activities throughout the Pacific Northwest, including climbing, hiking, backcountry skiing, snowshoeing, bicycling, camping, paddling, and more. The Mountaineers also supports its mission through its publishing division, Mountaineers Books, and promotes environmental education and citizen engagement. For more information, visit The Mountaineers Program Center, 7700 Sand Point Way NE, Seattle, WA 98115-3996; phone 206-521-6001; www.mountaineers .org; or email info@mountaineers.org.

Our publications are made possible through the generosity of donors and through sales of more than 700 titles on outdoor recreation, sustainable lifestyle, and conservation. To donate, purchase books, or learn more, visit us online.

MOUNTAINEERS
BOOKS

1001 SW Klickitat Way, Suite 201 • Seattle, WA 98134
800-553-4453 • mbooks@mountaineersbooks.org • www.mountaineersbooks.org

OTHER TITLES YOU MIGHT ENJOY FROM MOUNTAINEERS BOOKS

Pickets and Dead Men
Bree Loewen
Bree Loewen's first book is a chronicle of her three seasons as a climbing ranger, told with wry humor and honesty. "A gritty and revealing narrative from inside the belly of a tough beast, the National Park's ranger service on Mount Rainer." –Barry Blanchard

Sixty Meters to Anywhere
Brendan Leonard
Kinetic, funny, and heartfelt—a painfully honest story of a life changed by climbing. "A transformative personal journey, showing the power of climbing and the courage that lives within." –Kelly Cordes

Tilting at Mountains
Edurne Pasaban
A heartfelt and intimate account by the first woman to climb the world's fourteen 8000-meter peaks. "My real victory comes from both the effort and the prize, in the maturity and growth the challenge has provided me."

Mud Flats and Fish Camps
Erin McKittrick
A family of four, including two preschool-aged children, leaves the comforts of their yurt to hike and paddle the 800-mile coastline of Cook Inlet on a self-supported expedition of exploration, discovery, and challenge.

Mountains in my Heart
Gerlinde Kaltenbrunner
Effusive, charming, and tough, Gerlinde Kaltenbrunner climbed the fourteen 8000-meter peaks without high altitude porters or supplemental oxygen. "Up here, I am free; I can leave all responsibilities behind. I can be at one with myself."

My Old Man and the Mountain
Leif Whittaker
The son of the first American to reach the summit of Mount Everest, Leif Whittaker "writes much as he climbs mountains, with courage, grace, and a dash of humility. The result is an utterly compelling tale . . ." –Daniel James Brown

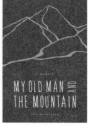

www.mountaineersbooks.org